STUDIES IN ECONOMICS AND POLITICAL SCIENCE

Volume 1

ENVIRONMENTAL PLANNING

ENVIRONMENTAL PLANNING

A Political and Philosophical Analysis

LINCOLN ALLISON

Routledge
Taylor & Francis Group

LONDON AND NEW YORK

First published in 1975 by George Allen & Unwin Ltd

This edition first published in 2022
by Routledge
4 Park Square, Milton Park, Abingdon, Oxon OX14 4RN

and by Routledge
605 Third Avenue, New York, NY 10017

Routledge is an imprint of the Taylor & Francis Group, an informa business

British Library Cataloguing in Publication Data
A catalogue record for this book is available from the British Library

ISBN: 978-1-03-212459-9 (Set)
ISBN: 978-1-00-322951-3 (Set) (ebk)
ISBN: 978-1-03-212430-8 (Volume 1) (hbk)
ISBN: 978-1-03-212465-0 (Volume 1) (pbk)
ISBN: 978-1-00-322464-8 (Volume 1) (ebk)

DOI: 10.4324/9781003224648

Publisher's Note
The publisher has gone to great lengths to ensure the quality of this reprint but points out that some imperfections in the original copies may be apparent.

Disclaimer
The publisher has made every effort to trace copyright holders and would welcome correspondence from those they have been unable to trace.

ENVIRONMENTAL PLANNING

A Political and Philosophical Analysis

Lincoln Allison
University of Warwick

London

GEORGE ALLEN & UNWIN LTD

RUSKIN HOUSE   MUSEUM STREET

ISBN 0 04 329021 3 hardback
ISBN 0 04 329022 1 paperback

Printed in Great Britain
in 10 point Plantin type
by T. and A. Constable Limited, Edinburgh

For
A. M. Mc.

PREFACE

This book is an essay on the relationship between environmental planning and political theory in Britain, though I hope it will be relevant to any society or to any situation in which there are environmental issues. Apart from its specific use for students of environmental planning and students of political theory, it is intended to interest anyone who is concerned with the relationship between political theory or philosophy and policy-making.

Because of the breadth of the subject-matter, I have not appended a bibliography; I hope that the notes will prove an adequate substitute. I have noted all references and sources which are essential to my analysis, except where a statement or argument is so widely quoted as to require no reference. I have sometimes used notes to make a point or to quote a passage which I consider to be relevant, but which would break up the thread of argument if incorporated into the text.

As this essay is the product of work begun (at Nuffield College, Oxford) in 1968 and continued throughout the period since, the number of people to whom I am indebted for information and stimulation is too large for me to mention individuals. A list, if constructed, would include politicians, planners, administrators, pressure-group officials and members of academic departments of Economics, History, Law, Literature, Management Science, Philosophy, Politics, Sociology and Town and Country Planning.

I would, however, like to thank the Department of Politics of the University of Warwick for allowing me to teach a course on the 'Political Aspects of Environmental Planning', and the students who have taken the course for the interest they have shown.

L. A.

CONTENTS

Chapter 1

The Environment
Fashion

This book is a sign of, and part of, a general intellectual concern about the relationship between man and his physical environment. The concern is not new; it has existed whenever and wherever there have been industrial development and urbanisation. But it has grown considerably in the industrial countries and Britain in particular since the mid-1960s. One aspect of the growth is that many people have rejected the established definitions of the important issues in politics. I myself reacted strongly in the mid- and late 1960s against what I took to be the triviality of contemporary political debate. The size and distribution of National Income—or baking and cutting of the 'National Cake' as it was often called—seemed to preoccupy politicians who paid little or no attention to the fundamental problems of environmental change. I soon discovered that my sentiments were neither new nor uncommon. Indeed, they had been forcibly expressed in 1929 by D. H. Lawrence in his essay, 'Nottingham and the Mining Country':

'The real tragedy of England, as I see it, is the tragedy of ugliness. The country is so lovely: the man-made England is so vile . . . make a new England. Away with little homes! Away with scrabbling pettiness and paltriness. Look at the contours of the land, and build up from these, with a sufficient nobility. The English may be mentally or spiritually developed. But as citizens of splendid cities they are more ignominious than rabbits. And they nag, nag, nag all the time about politics and wages and all that, like mean narrow housewives.'[1]

After about 1967 the emphasis changed. At least on the periphery of politics, in the media, the universities and among administrators there was something of an 'environment' fashion. By 1973 it was orthodox in polite circles to believe that population must be publicly controlled in the long run, and to claim that something must be done about the motor car. Ten years earlier the last of these beliefs was considered trivial and the first two were positively disreputable (though they were both over a century old).

It would be useful if social science could explain such changes in attitudes and beliefs, but we cannot do so with satisfactory precision. Causes and effects cannot be adequately distinguished: an influential book is probably both because it must be acceptable or plausible in order to be influential. We can, however, point to certain crucial landmarks. In 1967, E. J. Mishan's *The Costs of Economic Growth*[2] was published, explaining in lay terms the gist of more complex arguments he had put forward in his earlier essays on welfare economics. The prescriptive consequences of these arguments were to suspect economic and demographic growth and to emphasise the positive value of stability and of the quality of the environment. Elements of Mishan's theories can be found in some of the arguments in Frank Fraser Darling's 1969 Reith Lectures[3] or in Tony Aldous's *Battle for the Environment*,[4] published in 1972. Later one could hear the same arguments in Parliament or in *The Times* or on *Any Questions?* I don't know whether Fraser Darling or Aldous ever read Mishan, nor do I care; the diffusion of ideas is rarely as simple as a direct influence of one man on another. In other words, the complex relations between a variety of intellectual standpoints and the ways in which they are popularised in the media defy precision. Anyone who tried to analyse the 'permissive society' and the relationship between (say) Herbert Hart's essay, *Law, Liberty and Morality*,[5] and the reform of laws concerning homosexuality, abortion and divorce in the period 1964-70 must find the same problem: it is easy to point to landmarks, very difficult to assess their importance.

The contribution of the academic study of politics to the environment controversy has been slight; this is especially true of political theory. This paucity represents not merely a missed opportunity for scholars, but something of an intellectual catastrophe. Planning problems are misunderstood if they are thought of as technical problems to be solved by planners, architects, biologists, chemists or ecologists. As I shall argue in Chapter 2, they are really political problems in every sense. Because the dimension of political theory has been absent from much of the debate, there has been a mis-emphasis on the more melodramatic possibilities of environmental catastrophe: the 'Doomwatch Syndrome' as it has been called. The implication of the Syndrome is that we are faced with environmental catastrophe. Environmental issues are, therefore, technical. The goal is simple—survival—and the knowledge about how to survive is furnished by natural science. Managing the environment is thus no more political than keeping a car on the road.

There may be a problem about survival, about the persistence of the eco-system. But whether there is or isn't, in Britain there are many more complex issues and subtle dangers. These concern the availability of solitude, of peace and beauty, and of rewarding recreational activity. Life itself is not threatened, but some of its finer points are. My concern is that the genuine political problems—difficult problems of values and administration—might be ignored because environmental problems are equated with the Doomwatch Syndrome.

So this is a pretentious book. I am trying to place the more theoretical and value-laden problems of environmental planning in their philosophical and historical contexts. Inevitably, this involves taking sides, for some arguments are simply better than others. The main point is to analyse the arguments; the prescriptions are incidental. The pretension lies less in claiming to take a broader and more philosophical perspective than other writers on planning, than in actually trying to make the claim good. Think what it means to really understand planning. Geography, history, economics, politics, law, philosophy and sociology are all required to describe the human background. Geology, biology, chemistry and engineering describe the physical constraints. To understand what planners are doing requires some understanding of their cartographical and mathematical techniques. So there is no scope for intellectual modesty in writing about the relationship between man and environment.

The core of this book divides into three parts. Chapters 3-6 analyse the evolution of the planning system in the context of political and ideological developments. Chapters 7 and 8 outline fundamental positions in political theory as they can be applied to planning, while Chapters 9 and 10 analyse the role, potential as well as actual, of political action by private citizens in the planning process. In the historical section, Chapters 3 and 4, I shall take as my starting-point the two most important Acts of planning legislation—the Town Planning Act of 1909 and the Town and Country Planning Act of 1947. Neither was particularly controversial and I shall argue that they were commonly perceived as solutions to problems and that the problems were widely recognised as such by people of differing political views. However, I shall argue that the nature of each of the two Acts and their widespread acceptance must be understood in terms of deeper ideological movements. The last section of each of the two chapters examines these ideological components. Chapter 5 examines the working of the 1947 Act and the administrative machinery which it established. Chapter 6 deals with the strains on this machinery and the criticisms of it which were accumulating in the 1960s. Chapters 7 and 8 are the most important, because they emphasise the distinctive contribution of political theory to the understanding of environmental planning. In Chapter 7 I shall outline the main steps of the political theory which is predominant (though rarely fully articulated) in British administration; it is a modernised form of

Jeremy Bentham's 'greatest happiness' principle. I will distinguish between five interpretations of the principle. In Chapter 8 I will analyse some alternatives to the principle, five political theories, all relevant to planning, which fall completely outside the range of interpretation of the 'greatest happiness' principle. Chapter 9 examines a related aspect of the political theory of planning, the concept of public participation. I shall conclude that effective public participation usually involves organised groups and in Chapter 10 I will examine the nature and role of conservationist groups. Finally, in Chapter 11 I will argue that the principle of totemism, in many respects the precise opposite of the 'greatest happiness' principle, is relevant to planning and I will prescribe some practical applications of totemism.

It is important to relate the 'political' approach to environmental problems pursued in this book to the 'ecological' approach. Sir Frank Fraser Darling, a recognised ecologist, defines his subject as 'the science of the organism in relation to its whole environment, in relation to other organisms of different species, and to those of its own kind'.[6] In this strict sense, this book is about ecology. For although there is no discussion here of that most dramatic of ecological possibilities, the total breakdown of the eco-system, I am concerned with an aspect of ecology which is exclusively human. This book is about attempts by self-conscious, communicating beings to control their relationship to their environment and to define the principles which are to govern that relationship. That is to say, I am dealing with the special ecological situation of organisms with symbolic languages. The political part of the eco-system is not mainly concerned with the possible breakdown of the system as a whole, but with more subtle changes. In fact, Fraser Darling allots a special ecological role for politics: 'I think, indeed, that we need to develop some yardstick for human content; to be able to measure the lesser degree of discontent and psychosomatic disease in rehabilitated environments. This is the ultimate concern of politics.'[7] The validity and interpretation of this concept of politics are problems with which I will be constantly concerned in this book.

NOTES

1. *Phoenix: The Posthumous Papers of D. H. Lawrence* (London, Heinemann, 1936), p. 140.
2. E. J. Mishan, *The Costs of Economic Growth* (London, Staples, 1967).
3. Sir Frank Fraser Darling, *Wilderness and Plenty* (London and New York, Ballantine, 1971).
4. Tony Aldous, *Battle for the Environment* (Glasgow, Fontana, 1972).
5. H. L. A. Hart, *Law, Liberty and Morality* (Oxford, OUP, 1963).
6. Fraser Darling, op. cit., p. 9.
7. Ibid., pp. 30-1.

Chapter 2

The Politics of Planning

Environmental planning, the processes and patterns of action through which the use of land is controlled in a nation-state, is political. In the last few years this truth has become a kind of trivialised orthodoxy. By this I mean that the statement is made or admitted without its meaning being made clear or its implications realised. As with 'God is love' in theology, or an 'ought' cannot be inferred from an 'is' in moral philosophy, the statement is a sort of semantic dignified element formally stated but playing no real part in the argument. People say it, but then argue as if it were not the case. This is reflected in a great deal of writing about planning. There are conservationist tracts about planning, extended journalism (both good and bad) about planning, and technical and administrative debates about planning (by operational research experts and economists, for instance), but very little in the way of political analysis of planning, despite this widespread admission that planning involves 'politics'. However, the non-trivial implications of planning being 'politics' cannot be shown until we know what 'politics' is.

There have been many attempts by academic students of politics to define their subject-matter. Michael Oakeshott says: 'Politics I take to be the activity of attending to the general arrangements of a set of people whom chance or choice has brought together.'[1] Bernard Crick says: 'Politics, then, can be simply defined as the activity by which differing interests within a given unit of rule are conciliated by giving them a share in power in proportion to the welfare and survival of the whole community.'[2] To Robert Dahl: 'A political system is any persistent pattern of human relationships that involves, to a significant extent, power, rule or authority.'[3]

Most definitions juggle with some combination of concepts involving power, authority, order, organisation, rules and conflict. All of the three

B

above, and many more, seem fairly sensible without having strong claims to primacy. But none makes a really important distinction between political and non-political activity. Oakeshott's is too broad: it is important that not all attending to social arrangements is political. The distinction between politics and non-politics is an important one *between* forms of attending to social arrangements. Crick is far too narrow; his implication is that only certain more or less successful social arrangements, not common in the real world, contain politics. Dahl is also too narrow, but in a different dimension for he is restricting politics to the set of relationships which can be analysed in terms of certain highly dubious concepts.

There are two limiting questions which together can give us some lead into the nature of politics. Do creatures other than man have politics? Are there societies without politics? In both cases the most tempting answer is, 'It all depends on what you mean by politics', an answer which is often mistakenly identified with something called 'linguistic philosophy'. The debate need not end there, in semantic arbitrariness, for there are sensible and non-sensical distinctions to be made between politics and non-politics. A good distinction needs to satisfy two conditions: it must fall within the constraints of the majority of coherent usages of the word in the natural language (that is, it must be a definition of 'politics' and not of anything else), and it must allow us to say something which is not trivial.

Creatures other than man do not have political relations because political relations are one facet of social relations. Social relations exist only when there are two or more entities involved in a pattern of action which precludes their complete autonomy and which involves their consciousness of one another. The criterion of consciousness is symbolic communication; unless we can find evidence that beings communicate symbolically we cannot argue that they are conscious. No creatures other than human beings that we know of communicate symbolically as far as we know. Many other species have signal communications. That is, they affect each other's behaviour in systematic ways by patterns of behaviour which can be called communication. But they never say anything, they never argue, they have no concepts. If we did discover, perhaps on another planet, creatures who did communicate symbolic-ally—and we would only know if we could translate their symbolism (a process which must be possible if they were actually saying anything)—we should have to treat them as human. So in two senses, only human beings have social relations: of all the creatures we know only *homo sapiens* communicates symbolically and if we discovered another species with whom we could communicate symbolically we should recognise its members as essentially human.

This is not to say that men are not animals, but it is to say that men are not mere animals. Their behaviour has a dimension which other behaviour lacks in that it is also action. Action is behaviour by an actor; it is necessarily guided by a conscious mind. We understand both what an action is ('He put the kettle on'—function, purpose, decision) and why it has taken place ('because he wanted a cup of tea') in terms of the actor's state of mind. Only analogously or improperly do we understand animal behaviour in this way. To talk of the 'Social Life of the Termites' as some do, is incorrect, though not necessarily disastrously so; it remains a trivial mistake so long as there is no anthropomorphism in description or explanation.

So far I have talked about the nature of social relations. This is because politics is one factor in social relations or, to put this another way, the first part of a definition of politics is the same as a definition of social relations. At this point some theorists, including many Marxists, would stop, arguing that all social relations are political, distinctions between politics and other forms of social relation only serving to mislead. In doing so they fail to make an important distinction, between monolithic and schismatic societies. Only the latter have politics; at least the possibility of disagreement about the arrangement of social relations must exist before they are political. It is important to state this condition in terms of disagreement and not in terms of conflict as, for instance, does J. D. B. Miller.[4] Firstly, conflict is a behavioural word and as applicable to animals as to men. Secondly, conflict among men is quite possible without disagreement, and such conflict is essentially dissimilar to the range of action that can usefully be put within the bounds of politics. One interesting example is given by Alasdair MacIntyre talking about the Icelandic Sagas.[5] In the Sagas, it is possible for two Icelanders, in full obedience to the rules of kinship, to fight to the death without disagreeing about anything. They agree about the rules, they agree about the facts, both agree what must be done next, it is only a question of who will win the physical struggle.

This is to treat the society of the Icelandic Sagas as a monolithic morality within which there is no disagreement on rules, norms, values or procedures. Politics is not compatible with a monolithic morality. If a monolithic morality is possible, then so is an a-political society. Monolithic moralities are certainly *conceivable* and it seems reasonable to suppose that they have existed. The most promising cases are to be found in forms of simple communism and of absolute autocracy. In that sense my second limiting question has a clear answer: there can be societies without politics. Only perhaps in New Guinea and similar places might they be found at the present time.

Finally, politics involves a system of rules which has at least some tendency to persist and which provides partial procedures for the resolution of disagreement. Without this condition disagreement in a social context can dissolve into war or anarchy, both of which are essentially a-political.

THE NATURE AND FORMS OF DISAGREEMENT

I have argued that human conflict is possible without disagreement and that politics requires disagreement. Disagreement between two persons involves their holding contradictory propositions; it is not sufficient for them to have incompatible goals. In short, something must be at stake beyond what Brian Barry calls 'privately oriented wants'. Barry defines these as 'evaluations with oneself or one's family as their object'.[6] It is a rather poor definition of what is basically a very good distinction. Why, for instance, treat 'wants' as forms of evaluation? A want can be quite a primitive emotion which involves no evaluating; a dog can want its dinner without evaluating anything, so, for that matter, can I. It would seem more plausible, more in line with the natural language, to treat 'evaluations' as a sub-class of 'wants'. A better definition of privately oriented wants might be: X's privately oriented wants are those of his wants which are not rationally dependent on benefits to others, which can be fully and coherently expressed without reference to others.

Publicly oriented wants are those which are rationally dependent on benefits to others. Barry's account of these is much more satisfactory; he divides them into want-regarding publicly oriented wants and ideal-regarding publicly oriented wants. He seems to equivocate on the question of whether principles are the same thing as publicly oriented wants.[7] As far as I am concerned they are the same; a principle is simply a publicly oriented want and there is a useful distinction between ideal-regarding principles and want-regarding principles. In Barry's account:

'Want-regarding principles, then, are principles which take as given the wants people happen to have and concentrate attention entirely on the extent to which a certain policy will alter the overall amount of want-satisfaction or on the way in which the policy will alter the distribution among people of opportunities for satisfying wants.'[8]

Ideal-regarding principles are the remainder, those which concentrate attention on some idea of benefit to people which is not reducible to want-satisfaction or opportunities for satisfying wants.

These distinctions may seem trivial or irrelevant to the subject-matter of this book or they may seem common sense or they may seem both. On the contrary, they are not widely made; arguments become mystified because they are not; and the distinctions are particularly crucial to the understanding of environmental planning. Barry refers to 'the power of the distinction [between want-regarding and ideal-regarding principles] to illuminate political controversies whose foundations are at present obscure'.[9] I would make the claim particular: it is an especially useful distinction for understanding what is at stake between 'conservationists' and their opponents.

Let us take a very simple case of land-use control. A man, A, has a house which is next to a field owned by another man, B. B wants to build a factory in the field. Existing plans neither strongly encourage nor strongly discourage such a development. The decision is in the hands of the local planning authority, C. A objects to the proposal. There are three kinds of objections he could have:

1. *Privately oriented wants.* A wants the field to remain in its present state for what we would ordinarily call 'purely personal' reasons. He likes looking at it; he likes taking his dog for a walk in it. But simply by wanting the development not to take place he is not disagreeing with anyone. B might well take the attitude that obviously A is the last person who would want the development. If he wrote to C announcing that he did not want the development it could reasonably reply that it was not its job to satisfy his wants. He can only seriously object by producing a principle of the form, 'The development should not take place, because . . .' It is not only bad tactics for A to confine his expressions to his privately orientated wants; it also confines him to a passive role in political controversy. We can talk of the privately oriented wants of a group *qua* group as well as of individuals.

2. *Publicly oriented, want-regarding wants.* A may object to the development on the grounds that many people will be deprived of sources of want-satisfaction by it. He may argue that there is evidence for the amount of want-satisfaction in the numbers of people who walk, sit, picnic, fly kites and so on in the field.

3. *Publicly oriented, ideal-regarding wants.* A may claim that the sort of benefits which are fostered by the field being preserved are not adequately reflected by existing wants. He might say that as they consisted of beauty, solitude or academic interest they were not comparable with other wants. More extremely, he might argue that the development should be prevented despite public apathy or even enthusiasm for it on the grounds that the field was good for people in some way they did not themselves understand.

Only 2 and 3 allow of public argument. I shall argue in Chapters 7 and 8 that in our culture arguments of the 2-form are much more readily accepted than those of the 3-form. Statements of type-1 are not political arguments at all.

This simple example lacks many features of the real world. Normally, the debate would be much more likely to be about which field the factory should go in or what restrictions should be placed on building rather than whether it should go in a field at all. In practice, A would argue as if he had a type-2 want even if his real want was predominantly type-1 or type-3. But these factors are not really relevant; they only complicate the basic issue without changing it. That issue is about what sort of arguments can be used for and against development.

CONSERVATION AS PRINCIPLE AND THEORY

Conservation is political or social action in defence of the physical environment and levels of social benefit determined by that environment. Typically these benefits are hygienic, aesthetic or recreational and there may be intra-conservationist disagreements either about the interpretation of these values or about their relative importance. Properly, then, conservationism is a set of political principles, though not necessarily a particular set of principles, because the importance of preserving a given environment can be argued in many ways. We should distinguish in practice between genuine conservationism (the sincere holding of either want-regarding or ideal-regarding conservationist principles) and superficial conservationism where privately oriented dislike of particular developments is disguised by a set of principles. Often nationally based amenity groups can be categorised as genuine, and locally based groups as superficial. The test is to ask whether the opponents of development would continue to be politically active against it if its site were radically changed. The real motto of many local groups ought to be 'Not here, Oh Lord, not here'.

CONSERVATION AS POLITICAL THEORY

By definition, conservationism must involve a set of political principles. The kind of principles involved may be fairly simple evaluations with only one or two steps in the argument ('Nobody has a right to build roads so near people's houses; it is just not fair'). But at the other end of a scale of complexity, they may be part of, or derived from, political theories. By political theories, I mean theories of man's nature and legitimate ends in society which are relevant to any appraisal of governments and policies. Admittedly, this definition is an interpretation of the old-fashioned (yet still largely orthodox) usage of the expression 'political theories' in which they have a dimension of metaphysics and principles not necessarily possessed by all theories about politics. Analyses of political situations, or methodological arguments about how to study politics, or explanatory theories about politics, are not political theories in this traditional sense. However, they are sometimes called political theory, particularly in the United States. For example, not very much material in the admirable set of essays edited by David Easton, *'Varieties of Political Theory'*,[10] would be political theory in my sense.

Political theory can be studied in terms of its history; the context, development and effects of political ideas in a society over time. It can also be studied in terms of its structure—the logic, or 'conceptual geography', of political ideas and arguments. In my experience, teachers of political theory sometimes divide quite sharply in their emphasis, some tending to take the 'classics' of political thought as arguments to be analysed and criticised in terms of their logical coherence, while others prefer a more historical approach. In examinations one can ask, 'Did Locke have a coherent theory of property?' or 'Was Locke a theorist of the bourgeois revolution?'—two very different kinds of question. I am not suggesting that all analysts of political theory fall rigidly into one of these two categories, nor that logical and historical accounts of theory are completely irrelevant to one another, but I am arguing that they are separate exercises, even if they are conducted simultaneously on occasions (sometimes from necessity, but sometimes with mystifying effect). Both studies of political theory have a great deal to offer for the understanding of planning.

The relationship between the history of ideas and the history of planning is the starting-point of such a contribution. Even if one were only interested in the understanding of the planning process as it exists in the 'present', to attempt such an understanding without knowledge of the perspective, the context and the analogies furnished by the past relationship would be an exercise of dubious value. Not that there exists any one-way 'causal' relation between the development of political ideas and the development of planning. On the contrary, as we shall see, the gradual establishment of control over the environment of the urban proletariat in the nineteenth century in England can be said to have taken place despite persistent failure to construct a good theoretical argument for such control. Equally, where the relationship between environmental ideas and political theory was most explicit as with the 'Utopian' Socialists (Owen and Saint-Simon) in the early part of the century or the early urban sociologists (Geddes, Branford, Thomson) in the later part, the direct 'influence' of theory and theorists was least. Indeed, we can best understand some of the history of nineteenth-century environmental policy in terms of a fracturing of links between theory and policy. Nevertheless, the historical development of planning can only be understood in terms of the historical development of political ideas, for even where the two stories seem quite unconnected, the theoretical situation furnishes constraints, forms of argument and limiting cases for the policy situation.

When we move to the contemporary relationship between political theory and environmental issues, the importance of the connection becomes more clearly apparent. In talking of the issues of our own period, we are not merely interested in analysing what a relationship is, but also what it ought to be. If there is a lack of coherence here and now in the relationship between values, arguments and policies, the political theorist should point to it; this is obviously a less fruitful exercise when applied to past situations. For past cases, we can only improve our understanding of events by discerning intellectual incoherence; for the present case one cannot avoid influencing the very perceptions one describes, unless one has the misfortune to fall 'stillborn from the press'. The long history of the Third London Airport as an issue is a good example of how academic professors (Buchanan, Self, Hall, for instance), theoretical critiques of how the policy-making process appeared to be working, have influenced the same process at a later stage. Neither a contemporary political analyst nor a future historian could explain the policy outcome without first understanding the theoretical problems.

The political theorist's job in analysing a planning system is largely the job of explaining the operative concepts and values of modern planning in their relation to more widely used concepts and values and the forms in which both occur in argument. This is true of the 'participation' issue in planning, of the relation between values and 'expertise' in decision-making, and of the general analysis of needs and priorities in planning. In all these cases there are ongoing debates which lack, at present, the logical and historical perspectives which political theory should give them. The central theoretical issue, I shall argue, is the structure of want-regarding principles and their role in furnishing planning criteria. Can want-regarding principles be effectively distinguished? What is their common structure? What forms of want-regarding principle are there? Do they, as I would claim, have a *de facto* primacy in contemporary administration? What arguments remain for allowing ideal-regarding principles to override want-regarding principles? What kinds of ideal are relevant to planning? These questions of political theory are also vital planning questions for the nature, purpose and methods of the planning system should stem from the answers. Both critical and explanatory arguments about planning require political theory.

POLITICAL SCIENCE AND ITS CONTRIBUTION

I have argued that planning, its historical development and its current issues, can only be understood in terms of political theory. But the study of politics can contribute to the understanding of planning in other ways, ways which fall outside my definition of 'theory'. The other part of the study of politics, normally covered by one or all of the words 'behaviour', 'institutions' or 'systems', also has a contribution to make. For if my argument for the relevance of political theory is correct, it follows also that planning processes can be understood as political institutions and that actions within the planning process can be observed and correlated as political behaviour. Examples of potentially useful accounts of planning as political institutions are easy to find: case studies of planning controversies, assessments of the role of pressure groups on planning, investigations of the relationship (possibly in 'power' and 'influence' terms) between professional officials of planning departments and elected councillors, comparative studies of planning processes in developed countries—the USA, Britain, France, West Germany, for instance. There are more: the public inquiry as a political institution, the sociological properties of active conservationists, the socialisation process as it affects attitudes to environmental issues. All these are fascinating and important questions. Indeed, I have found it necessary to touch on most of them in this book, but without doing the detailed research that would provide really useful information. In all cases they can be investigated untheoretically, though I would still claim they were best understood in the perspective of political theory.

The outstanding issue remains as to the nature of the relationship between such institutional or behavioural studies and theoretical analysis. I would claim that they are interdependent, though this claim does not imply that an institutional study depends for its validity on a particular political theory. But what of the traditional alternative claim, that there can be a science of politics independent of political theories and evaluations? In one clear and strong sense of 'science' this claim is nonsense. 'Science' in its purest sense is the theoretical investigation of the causal regularities of the universe. In this sense, only theoretical physics is a science. But the more common sense, of explanatory disciplines reducible in principle to the fundamental relations of the universe, also excludes politics. Chemistry, mechanics, physiology are all reducible to and logically connected with, fundamental physical theory. Politics is not; it is part of a social discourse in which entities are conceived and understood in terms of their consciousness. Of course these entities are also physical objects—human beings are also members of the species *homo sapiens*. But that has nothing to do with politics. Neurophysiological or chemical accounts of Cabinet members are possible, and part of science; they do not advance our understanding of Cabinet government at all. The language of consciousness and the ways in which we try to understand the collective and individual actions of people in a social context, is a separate discourse from the language of science, even though the two languages can be used to describe the same event. My brain consists of energy-in-space; it is a proper object of scientific inquiry. My mind consists of a history of consciousness which can only be understood on its own terms. Because there is a logically separate discourse for understanding social behaviour, it is a confusion to describe politics as a 'science'. The confusion can be trivial. After all, many of the thousands of 'political scientists' in the world act exactly as they would if they were called political analysts or contemporary political historians. But it can also be a dangerous confusion where it directs the political scientist on a quest for law-like regularities or behavioural correlations at the expense of real social understanding.

Calling politics a 'science' can, I suppose, have the relatively harmless role of stating an aspiration: that the study of politics should be coherent, logical and produce statements which are 'causally adequate' in Max Weber's sense (which means checkable by some fairly precise procedure). As an aspiration, this is admirable until it comes to involve a preference for measurable concepts over unmeasurable regardless of their real virtue in providing insight or, more extremely, 'statistical positivism',[11] the rejection of statements without implications for measurement.

This old and rather thorny debate about the study of politics has already entered the arguments about planning and politics. Roy Gregory's book, *The Price of Amenity*,[12] is one of the very few books about planning by an academic student of politics. The bulk of the book consists of five detailed case studies of planning controversies. Neither the style, nor the content, of these case studies make concessions to 'scientific' politics. He refers to the case studies as a 'collection of stories',[13] and argues that:

'. . . it is hard to see how the somewhat indeterminate variables that characterise administrative situations could ever be rigorously and scientifically controlled, or how hypotheses could ever be systematically tested without replicating an enormous number of cases so much alike as to become insufferably boring.'[14]

It is not that the 'stories' are isolated narratives; they have a unity, but a unity which cannot be expressed in terms of behavioural variables.

'Each of the five controversies described in the following chapters has its own special features and its own particular flavour. Yet however much situations may differ in detail, the underlying configuration of interests, strategies and perspectives seems to remain much the same.'[15]

Gregory does not specifically argue, but he does imply, that it is the theoretical and ideological perspectives which really get us 'in' to the planning process:

'To put himself in the shoes of those involved in a controversy, the reader must know something of their institutional responsibilities and perspectives; he must take account of the pressures and constraints that they had to contend with, and he must himself grapple with the facts and arguments presented to the men who had to make the decisions.'[16]

The main step one can take in understanding the planning process is to understand the theoretical context in which planning arguments take place. Any attempt to analyse the 'behaviour' of those involved in the process or in controversies without a theoretical understanding cannot succeed.

In fact, this is the sort of conclusion that Gregory comes to, without really noticing its nature. The constant theme he observes in planning controversies is the attempt to make (and rationalise) choices between sets of benefits whose financial value can be calculated ('developments') and sets of benefits whose social value is thought to lie beyond financial calculation:

'If there is one persistent and blindingly obvious motif that runs through all amenity disputes, it is clearly this: what we are not prepared to pay for, we cannot have. But who are "we"? And how do "we" decide what is to be spent on preserving or enhancing amenity and the natural environment?'[17]

Thus Gregory's title, *The Price of Amenity*. I intend to further this understanding and to show that the key to planning lies in contemporary theoretical orthodoxy and the forms of its want-regarding emphasis.

Of course, Gregory has been attacked for his lack of science. In a review article about the problem of case studies and Gregory in particular, Adrian Webb criticises those who are 'pessimistic' about the possibility of scientific case studies. They 'go further and argue that because of the number of variables that must be controlled, political phenomena *per se* are not amenable to scientific study, although they admit that case studies can be used to give and refine "leads". Gregory seems to be a pessimist. . . .'[18] Webb's own suggestions are vague; he wants 'control' comparisons where only some variables change between sets of cases, he wants a 'systematic' treatment of cases, and he wants individual cases to be seen in relation to models of a more general policy process. Some of his statements are rather odd: '. . . without concepts the data lack form or substance and it is impossible to assess which data the author has consistently included and which he may have neglected.'[19] No political statements can be made 'without concepts' and Gregory's analysis certainly has plenty. Webb obviously means by concepts the sort of concepts which are claimed to be 'scientific'.

Quite independent of any evidence, Webb asserts:

'The strength of the amenity argument is determined by the number, size, prestige and tactical skill of the supporting interest groups and the resources they commit to voicing it.'[20]

He appears not to have noticed that Gregory's stories specifically preclude that claim if it is interpreted as meaning that planning controversies are won by the side with most measurable 'resources'. Planning controversies are won by arguments judged within a limited range of (want-regarding) political principles and theories. Only if 'tactical skill' is given primacy in Webb's account and interpreted largely in terms of weak and strong arguments, can Webb's statement be true. And that interpretation would again lead us away from Webb's 'variables' and in the direction of understanding contemporary political theory.

CONCLUSION

Planning is political action. This means it can only be properly understood in the context of current political principles and theories. The untheoretical study of politics can also contribute to the understanding of planning, but only if it is interpreted modestly as a limited form of analysis which complements the analysis of planning as political theory.

NOTES

1. Michael Oakeshott, 'Political Education', in Peter Laslett (ed.), *Philosophy, Politics and Society* (Oxford, Blackwell, 1956), p. 2.
2. Bernard Crick, *In Defence of Politics* (London, Pelican, 1964), p. 21.
3. Robert A. Dahl, *Modern Political Analysis* (Prentice-Hall, 1963), p. 6.
4. J. D. B. Miller, *The Nature of Politics* (London, Pelican, 1965), pp. 13-23.
5. MacIntyre's analysis of the Icelandic Sagas was contained in his series of lectures, *What was Morality?*, delivered at the University of Oxford in 1965. I was surprised to find it totally absent from his book, *A Short History of Ethics* (London, Routledge, 1967).
6. B. M. Barry, *Political Argument* (London, Routledge, 1965), p. 12.
7. Ibid., pp. 38-41, 71-2.
8. Ibid., p. 38.
9. Ibid., loc. cit.
10. David Easton (ed.), *Varieties of Political Theory* (Prentice-Hall, 1966).
11. John Rex, Professor of Sociology at the University of Warwick, is the author of this phrase.
12. Roy Gregory, *The Price of Amenity: Five Studies in Conservation and Government* (London, Macmillan, 1971).
13. Ibid., p. 307.
14. Ibid., p. xiiin.

15. Ibid., p. 35.
16. Ibid., p. xiii.
17. Ibid., p. 296.
18. Adrian Webb, 'Planning Inquiries and Amenity Policy', in *Policy and Politics*, Vol. 1, No. 1 (1972), p. 65.
19. Ibid., p. 66.
20. Ibid., p. 70.

Chapter 3

The Idea of Town Planning before 1909

Any account of the development of planning in Britain must start with the Town Planning Act of 1909. This is not because the Act represents the beginning of the planning machinery we now know: what it established was far too partial to be recognisable as modern planning machinery. Nor is it because it represented a legislative beginning to the idea of planning: it would be fairer to place such a beginning somewhere amongst the public health and housing legislation of the Victorian period. The 1909 Act can best be seen as a midway point, a careful contrast with both the planning machinery which has existed since 1947 and with all that had been called the planning of towns before.

What the Act did was to provide for local authorities to produce schemes for controlling the development of new housing areas. The purpose of these schemes was described as 'securing proper sanitary conditions, amenity and convenience' in future housing development. What it did not do, in terms of modern planning, requires considerably more statement. It did not allow local authorities to institute any overall planning; the idea, essential to modern planning, of the comprehensive strategy—the 'development' or 'structure' plan in the UK or the 'master' plan in the USA—was to remain a creation of isolated individuals such as Geddes and Abercrombie until 1947. So no planning profession was created. Instead of a new type of public employee there were more extensive tasks for existing public employees including surveyors, engineers and architects. There was no provision for planning non-urban areas, though there had been concern about the effects of urbanisation and change on the countryside throughout the Victorian period and Lord Meath had already suggested the idea of a green 'belt round London.[1] There was no provision for controlling what happened in the areas which were already urbanised and, in any case, planning was a possibility for a local authority rather than a duty. Finally, and perhaps most indicative, there was no machinery for compensation and betterment although it had been realised since Haussmann's reconstruction of central Paris after 1848 that these were fundamental problems of any public control of land use. Any land-use planning which actually prohibits people from doing with their land what they would otherwise have done, raises issues of compensation. Conversely, many public projects will effectively put money into the pockets of certain private individuals by 'bettering' their surroundings and facilities.

What then was new about the 1909 Act? The idea of town planning was very old indeed; Abercrombie's book[2] on the subject begins with Mesopotamia on the fringes of prehistory. Many towns had been comprehensively planned for a complex of social and political purposes in the years since. Colin and Rose Bell's book, *City Fathers*,[3] which deals with town planning in Britain before the 'Town Planning Movement', gives many examples of 'plantation' towns. According to the Bells, every major town in Wales has its origins as a planned town rather than as an organic development. In any case, the building and sanitation legislation of the previous forty years already constituted partial land-use control. The 'by-law' housing which had been constructed under this legislation was quite different from, and hygienically superior to, the housing of the earlier period.

But the 1909 Act was something new in that it was an attempt on a national scale to use the control of land use for the solution of a major social problem, the condition of the urban proletariat. Previous comprehensive town planning had included (throughout recorded history) the construction of public works for glory and as symbols of the aspirations of a group, a society or a man. There had been projects to design pleasant environments for the upper classes. Colonialists—whether the English in Wales or the Romans throughout their empire—had designed towns to play a part in the economic and military control of the colonised territory. Individual capitalists from Owen onwards had attempted to improve the condition of their work forces through solutions which were largely environmental. But there had never before been an attempt to set up physical controls of future building so as to improve the conditions of the poor and the stability of the whole society.

The Act was not a controversial measure, especially in comparison with the other interventionist measures passed by Liberal governments between 1906 and 1914. Unlike the Shops Act of the same year or the introduction of old age pensions two years later, it did not seem to strike drastically at any particular group, either at their principles or at their purses. Lyttleton, as Conservative spokesman on Local Government Board matters, did not oppose the measure on principle; he confined himself to querying its effectiveness. However, my opinion of the significance of the Bill as a new form of social organisation was shared by its proposer, John Burns, who said: 'The object of the Bill is to provide a domestic condition for the people in which their physical health, their morals, their character and their whole social condition can be improved by what we hope to secure in this Bill.'

The lack of opposition can be superficially explained in terms of a number of cultural conditions. The Act was seen as a sensible solution to a practical problem. As Burns pointed out, the previous fifteen years had seen a considerable urbanisation of rural land on the fringes of large towns and cities, the total was estimated to be over half a million acres. This was a process which, as Burns put it: 'We have no right to allow to proceed unregulated.' Neither party contained sufficiently large numbers of ideologists who objected to such regulation to provide any weight of opposition on principle. Indeed, British parties have rarely contained important groups of ideological intellectuals and no subsequent planning legislation has been firmly opposed on political principle. Crucially, perhaps, the 'experts' were for the Act; few if any of those intimately connected with housing, architecture or urban problems did not regard it as at least a step in the right direction.

PRESSURE FOR REFORM: THE TOWN PLANNING MOVEMENT

Behind Parliament's acceptance of the new planning lay a moderate alliance of local politicians, professionals in the intellectual skills related to housing and local government, intellectuals and businessmen. It was moderate in that clear-cut notions of what ought to be done (such as Ebenezer Howard's view that the old urban centres must eventually be abandoned in favour of purpose-built 'garden cities') and theories of why it should be done (such as Patrick Geddes's ideas of civic sociology) were transcended in the interests of immediate, if petty, reform. It was an alliance because it included divergent views as to how far planning should go as well as very different conceptions of the problems which planning was to solve. It was given an organisational form in the National Housing Reform Council, which was founded in 1900.

A number of the 'enlightened' capitalists were supporters, including members of the Cadbury, Lever and Rowntree families. Cadbury's had founded Bournville on the garden city model in 1878 and Lever had established Port Sunlight in 1887. Seebohm Rowntree had been active in the investigation of the conditions of the poor and in the improvement of housing conditions in York since the 1890s. Among a number of local politicians, inspired by both local successes and local frustrations to press for national action, the most well-known were J. S. Nettlefold, Chairman of Birmingham City Housing Committee, and William Thompson, an alderman of Richmond, Surrey. Both these men had been instrumental in improving housing conditions in their areas; both felt that the work could not be advanced unless local authorities were empowered to exercise control in the way in which new housing projects were constructed. Ashworth stresses the importance of a number of professional organisations which supported the Council and gave it evidence and credibility;[4] these included the Royal Institute of British Architects, the Surveyors Institute and the Association of Municipal and County Engineers.

It is more difficult to typify the role or the motivation of the intellectuals in the movement. Academically the most impressive was Patrick Geddes, but he was also the most mysterious and complex. It is difficult even to say what Geddes was; he was part biologist, part sociologist and part planner, but had many other interests. His aspiration was to synthesise these interests into a treatise on sociology, but the treatise was never written. He tried to envisage cities as systematic wholes and to inter-relate their physical, artistic, economic, social and moral lives. This attempt culminated in his book, *Cities in Evolution*, published in 1911. His ultimate concern was with the quality of life in cities. Geddes's theories and preoccupations gave him a completely different outlook from many people in the Town Planning Movement who had a much narrower intellectual interest and approach to problems: viz. architecture and the ways in which it could be used to solve specific problems. One Geddes scholar has summed up this relationship as follows:

'Controlling the form of cities was left to the small but developing band of town planners. For them Geddes's work was very important indeed. Apart from the odd Utopian-like Ebenezer Howard, the men drawn into planning were mainly architects. Geddes's *Civics: as applied sociology* was a straw that they could grasp at, aware that their work had sociological implications, but not knowing ultimately what these were. . . . He voiced the need for a sociological understanding of city development. But it remains true that in respect of technique and method as to how this should be achieved, his two papers on *Civics: as applied sociology* were in reality a beautiful backwater as far as the future of both sociology and town planning were concerned.'[5]

I would go further than this and argue that Geddes's preoccupation with understanding the city systematically and totally in all its contexts, as well as his emphasis on quantifying variables relevant to the quality of life, is far closer to some of the most modern, and American, techniques of planning (such as mathematical systems analysis). It was far less relevant to the generation after 1909. Planning remained primarily architectural; witness, for instance, Thomas Sharp's book, *Town and Country Planning*, written in 1939, which shows considerable evidence

C

of a belief in the importance of aesthetics and architecture and very little emphasis on sociology.

Ebenezer Howard, too, can be quite properly accused of a belief in architectural determinism. His book, *Tomorrow*,[6] assumes that if the conditions in which people live can be improved, all other social problems can be dealt with. In its extreme form, his prescription was that all existing conurbations should be abandoned and people moved into attractive garden cities. When Geddes read his paper, *Civics: As Applied Sociology*, to the newly formed Sociological Society in 1904, Howard told him that his conceptions of both history and geography were misplaced. According to Howard, Geddes did not realise that urbanisation was destroying 'more and more the beautiful fields and hilly slopes . . . [making] the atmosphere more foul and the task of the social reformer more and yet more difficult'.[7] There is no doubt in my mind that though Geddes was by far the more intellectually impressive of the two, Howard had, by as great a margin, the better of it when we come to estimate influence. Howard's achievement was that he applied some of the deepest Victorian objections to contemporary urbanisation and industrialism (latent or manifest in so much of the art and literature of the period) into a simple ideal: the garden city. Further diluted, this ideal had considerable impact on architecture and planning, with effects that can be seen still.

In the case of many of the other intellectuals who could be said to have influenced town planning, their conception of the nature of the problem was more specific. Of the more specific problems, physical health was the most urgent and important. In 1871, Dr H. W. Rumsey had written *On a Progressive Physical Degeneracy of Race in the Town Populations of Great Britain*,[8] but the real facts came to be taken seriously only with the Boer War when it was discovered that many recruits from the industrial areas were too weak physically to make effective soldiers—in some cases too weak to use a rifle. This discovery led to the establishment of the Inter-Departmental Committee on Physical Deterioration. The Committee could find no clear evidence of an unsatisfactory state of health. This was the consequence of the very nature of the slum areas, it reported, and these would continue to proliferate unless local authorities could be given powers to control new building. The 1909 Act was thus a recommendation of the Committee. T. C. Horsfall used the public health evidence to argue that Britain's position in comparison to Germany was at stake: we could not afford to allow prevailing urban conditions to continue if we were to compete, militarily or economically, with Germany. He put this case in his book, *The Relation of Town Planning to National Life*, which was published in 1908. Those who believe that all or most human progress is the consequence of international competition can find some support in the development of town planning. Health, or 'racial fitness', presented a measurable problem, which linked directly with our place in international economic competition and with our potential for war.

THE INTELLECTUAL ORIGINS OF TOWN PLANNING

A one-dimensional account of the history of planning would be this: in reaction to the urban conditions following industrialisation, government slowly began to regulate environmental conditions; it began with limited and definite problems and expanded in territorial generality until comprehensive planning existed. Cullingworth has it: 'Town and Country Planning as a task of Government has developed from public health and housing policies.'⁹ The Public Health Act of 1848 provided for Local Boards of Health to be set up to regulate sanitary and sewage facilities. The Artisans and Labourers Dwellings Act of 1868 gave local authorities powers to regulate individual houses. The Artisans and Labourers Dwellings Improvement Act and the Public Health Act, both 1875, allowed authorities to control sanitary conditions in all areas and architectural features of new housing development. These were the predecessors of the 1909 Act, just as the 1947 Town and Country Planning Act is its logical successor because it established formal controls for the whole country and in much larger areas, the counties and county boroughs.

This is a useful framework on which to attach an understanding of planning. But it is only a framework; really to understand what happened involves an investigation of the theories and values which affected, on the one hand, the aspirations which men had for their environment and, on the other, the beliefs about how it could, or could not, be controlled. The whole of Victorian intellectual life was a reaction to industrialisation and especially to the existence of the industrial proletariat—a great unschooled, ungoverned, undrained and unpoliced mass, different in every way from the poor classes of previous times. The lives of Dickens and Disraeli, of Mill, Marx, Engels and Green, of Ruskin and Morris were largely attempts to adjust to this situation, unknown to their intellectually eminent predecessors. Fear of these masses, and concern for them, overshadowed any man who sought to be both intellectually and morally serious.

In trying to typify the main strains and themes in this concern, perhaps the best place to begin is with romanticism. 'Romanticism' is a difficult word; it has been used to mean an idea, a style, a period, a movement and other entities with precious little in common between them. When I say 'romantic', I mean possessing some combination of these attitudes: a belief that important actions and achievements were not wholly rational; a preference for rural over urban surroundings;

a belief that the past was at least partly superior to the present. Although primarily an artistic movement, romanticism both influenced and even became, social comment. Sometimes this social comment was wildly impractical: in William Morris's 1884 lecture, *Art and Socialism*, he proposed the rejection of all British industrialisation. Men were to return to their ancient crafts and to the land; Britain was to become a green garden. It is difficult to attribute any direct influence to what was, in practical terms, literally romantic nonsense. But indirectly the romanticism of Morris and of the artists and poets had a great influence. Through Howard (and others) it led to the rejection of the industrial city and the attempts to rurify the city—through parks, gardens, green belts and leafy suburbs. In the development of planning it has constantly furnished spiritual criticisms of the output of planning and, eventually, it provided the emotional force behind the movement to defend rural England. However, 'romanticism' in another aspect had a different impact on planning. Thomas Sharp, for instance, rejected D. H. Lawrence's accusation that the English had no urban tradition worthy of the name. According to Sharp, the cities of eighteenth-century England were the finest in Europe, but 'the Renaissance tradition did not last so long in England as it did elsewhere. It was a fine, singing, high-flying bird that was knocked to smithereens by two wretched missiles: one the smothering dough-lump of the Romantic Revival, the other the iron-hand money-bag of the Industrial Revolution.'[10]

The ideological form of this 'iron-hand money-bag' was *laissez-faire* political economy, the doctrine that the workings of the unregulated economy automatically maximised human well-being and that any attempt by governments to control these workings could only do harm where it had any effect whatsoever. The body of iron-law doctrine, developed by Adam Smith and the Scottish economists, continued by Jeremy Bentham and Herbert Spencer, and proselytised as a personal morality by Samuel Smiles, argued that theoretical moralising about what ought to be public policy was fundamentally irrelevant to social reality. Public policy could only direct economic resources with less efficiency than the interplay of private interests. Thus Herbert Spencer's opposition to the 1848 Public Health Act or the objections to it as a Bill expressed in *The Economist* of 13 May 1848:

'. . . suffering and evil are nature's admonitions; they cannot be got rid of; and the impatient attempts of benevolence to banish them from the world of legislation before benevolence has learned their object and end, have always been more productive of evil than good.'

Laissez-faire is the prime candidate for a 'prevailing ideology' in Britain in the century before 1909. Some have argued that it has been the main influence on our public policy. Certainly, as a theory it held sway throughout this period and later—possibly until the Second World War. I was taught something very much like it as a sixth-former in the 1960s. But I agree with Benevolo that *laissez-faire* political economy was often theoretically supreme without being universally influential in practice. It was over-ridden in the making of practical policy by an attitude which did not have the benefit of theoretical coherence. Benevolo calls this attitude 'Conservative Reformism' and argues that it was the most important policy-making attitude in Western Europe after 1848.[11] Conservative Reformism must be defined as a practical attitude: the belief that public policy could solve problems, that governments could make life in the cities better, irrespective of theories. Benevolo sums up the position of reforms in England when he describes the reaction of the protagonists of the 1848 Public Health Act to their economist critics: 'All Chadwick and his colleagues could set against these philosophical arguments was common sense and the undeniable reality of the epidemics rife in London at this time.'[12]

The greatest of English Conservative Reformers was Benjamin Disraeli. In his novels he was preoccupied with the existence of the urban proletariat and its disturbing exclusion from society. His novels, *Coningsby* and *Sybil* (sub-titled *The Two Nations*), are preoccupied with the situation of the industrial proletariat and openly encouraging of manufacturers who tried, as far as possible, to give their workers decent homes and gardens. Disraeli's novels and his political career are fully consistent. It is clear from both that he genuinely believed in the worth of the society in which he was living, and regarded the exclusion of the urban proletariat from the workings of that society as both bad and dangerous. In order to draw them into the fold he offered them not doctrinal equality, but political leadership and better living conditions.

Conservative Reformism can only be understood as a practical defence of society and as a reaction to the failure of theories to solve everyday problems. It connects, in a strange way, with a body of theory which sounds like its opposite: Utopian Socialism. By this I mean conceptions of ideal alternative societies (without necessarily any conception of how to achieve them), with architecture and social relations being causally connected facets of the difference between the existing society and the Utopian. Fourier, Owen and Saint-Simon have all been described as Utopian Socialists, but it was Robert Owen's practical humanisation of capitalists' action which had the real influence on planning. Owen's experiments at New Lanark suggested that it could be good business as well as good policy to improve working-class housing. His ideals were thus the fore-runners of the practical achievements of such capitalists as the Richardsons, the Levers and the Cadburys in improving the housing of their workers.

There were two kinds of motives for wanting to better the conditions of the poor: genuine concern and fear of the consequences of not doing so. It is as naïve to suggest that only the latter could have been effective as it is to suggest that it was mainly the former. In most cases the two motives are difficult to distinguish; indeed, in Disraeli's case, they were almost the same thing. Sometimes the attempt to buy off the working classes was fairly overt. Take the case of this report to the *Société Industrielle de Mulhouse* on the workers' housing project in that city in the 1850s:

'If we can offer these same men clean, attractive houses, if we can procure for each man a small garden, where he can find pleasant and useful employment, where caring for his own small harvest he can learn to value that feeling for ownership which Providence has instilled in us all, shall we not have solved one of the most important problems of social economy? Shall we not have contributed towards strengthening the sacred bonds of the family and rendered a true service to this class so worthy of concern, to our workers and to all society.'[13]

But even in this passage it is clear that conservative prudence and Utopian aspiration are inexorably intertwined.

It remains to mention Marxism. Marx and Engels were as knowledgeable and as concerned about the condition of the urban proletariat as anybody in the Victorian period, but they had no 'influence', as such, on the planning movement. Benevolo argues that they had an effect, though this was basically negative. Marxism diverted the energies of the 'left' in Europe after 1848—Marx attached Utopians and piecemeal reformers—and left social reform based on architecture as the prerogative of the 'right'.

OCTAVIA HILL: THE PARADIGM VICTORIAN

Men like Marx—or, for that matter, Geddes—who eventually appear prominently in the intellectual histories of their own age are usually neither influential in, nor typical of, their own times. In order to understand the main themes and preoccupations of the Victorian age, it is more useful to study Octavia Hill in whose life the contrasting theories and values can be observed.

Octavia Hill was born in 1838 and died in 1912. Her name is still slightly known, because she founded the National Trust in 1895. Her early ambition was to be an artist; at the age of 18 she was both pupil and assistant to John Ruskin. Ruskin encouraged her aspirations, but she came to find his unsatisfactory. One biographer[14] records this quaint conversation:

'Once he was complaining that he could no longer enjoy the Alps. Why should noble things lose their influence when they ceased to be fresh to us?

' "I can suggest one thing about delight," said Octavia. "Whenever we begin to think about our own feelings we cannot be happy."

' "But I have been thinking about mine ever since I went away, of little else. Dear me, that is quite a new thought to me."

'Octavia replied that "feelings, especially our own, are not fit aims for effort; they are not noble enough . . ."

'Ruskin confessed that he had no troubles; but the decay of sensibility to natural beauty had gone on. He wanted "larger Alps".

' "And do you think larger Alps would satisfy you?"

' "Not at all." '[15]

Later this dissatisfaction stimulated action.

'Ruskin was talking about the dreariness of life "with no object except the usual daily round" . . . "I paint ⟨ . . . I take my mother for a drive, dine with friends, or answer these correspondents."

'He drew a bundle of letters from his pocket and said wearily, "One longs to do something."

' "Most of us feel like that at times," replied Octavia drily—but her eyes were smiling.

' "Well . . . what would you like to be doing?" he asked.

' "Something to provide better homes for the poor," replied Octavia in a flash.

'Ruskin turned in his chair.

' "How could it be done? Have you a business plan?" '[16]

Miss Hill turned out to be a most practical woman. She succeeded in purchasing Paradise Place, a tenement court between Baker Street and Marylebone High Street. Here she operated as a normal landlord except that she did not try to maximise her profits, she did not employ middlemen to deal with her tenants, she supervised the maintenance of the homes herself, and she tried at all times to be personally friendly to her tenants. She would not tolerate arrears of rent; those who drank away their wages were evicted. Later she admitted that this was sometimes 'cruel', but there were good reasons for it. There were plenty of tenants wanting to come in and it was better to reward the deserving than the undeserving. In any case, as a woman she had to convince people of her ability to be practical rather than sentimental: all projects must be rooted in 'sound finance'.

Miss Hill was a successful organiser of housing projects, just as for the last thirty years of her life she was a successful campaigner to preserve open spaces and beauty spots in south-eastern England. Her houses became—and remained—cleaner, more hygienic, and less delinquent than their predecessors. In the course of her career she also played important parts in the expansion of universities and in the founding of the Army Cadet Corps. She loved nature and the countryside, and aspired to preserve them both really and artistically. At the same time she felt a need to help the urban poor which was more urgent and more overwhelming. She was concerned, too, with the position of women in society and she attempted to solve both these problems through that most eminently Victorian of activities, social work, and all this was done within the constraints of respectable morality and sound finance.

Octavia Hill was the paradigm Victorian. She was moved by all the forces which combined, and sometimes conflicted, in creating the idea of town planning.

NOTES

1. In *Sphere* (1901).
2. Patrick Abercrombie, *Town and Country Planning* (Oxford, OUP, 1933).
3. Colin and Rose Bell, *City Fathers* (Harmondsworth, Pelican, 1972).
4. William Ashworth, *The Genesis of Modern British Town Planning* (London, Routledge, 1954), Chap. 7.
5. H. E. Meller, 'Patrick Geddes: An Analysis of His Theory of Civics, 1880-1904', in *Victorian Studies*, Vol. 16, No. 3, p. 315.
6. Ebenezer Howard, *Tomorrow: A Peaceful Path to Real Reform*, published privately in 1898. Reprinted as *Garden Cities of Tomorrow* (London, 1902) and later edited by F. J. Osborn (London, Faber, 1946).
7. Meller, op. cit., p. 311. An account of the origins of the Sociological Society is given in R. J. Halliday, 'The Sociological Society and the Genesis of Academic Sociology in Britain', in *The Sociological Review*, Vol. 16, No. 3 (1968). Halliday distinguishes schools of 'ethical or social work sociologists ... civic sociologists or town planners ... [and] racial sociologists' of whom the first named became predominant in the movement.
8. In *Transactions of the National Association for Promotion of Social Science*.
9. J. B. Cullingworth, *Town and Country Planning* (London, Allen & Unwin, 1967), rev. edn, p. 15.
10. Thomas Sharp, *Town Planning* (London, Penguin, 1940), p. 17.
11. Leonardo Benevolo, *The Origins of Modern Town Planning*, translated by Judith Landry (London, Routledge, 1967).
12. Ibid., p. 98.
13. Quoted in J. B. Godin, *Solutions Sociales* (1871).
14. William Thomson Hill, *Octavia Hill* (London, Hutchinson, 1956).
15. Ibid., p. 52. These conversations are taken from Sir E. T. Cook's *The Life of Ruskin* (1912). They are not included in E. Moberley Bell, *Octavia Hill* (London, Constable, 1943), second impression (corrected), which otherwise presents a very similar account of Miss Hill's life.
16. Hill, op. cit., p. 56.

Chapter 4

Town and Country
Planning, 1909-1947

In 1913 a leader in the *Town Planning Review* said of the 1909 Act that 'few Acts of Parliament have created such universal appreciative interest and been launched with such promises of success'. By 1915 74 authorities had prepared 105 schemes covering 168,000 acres. The most spectacular single development was the creation of a 6,000-acre residential area in the Ruislip-Northwood area, north-west of London. Conditions were especially favourable in that district: the Central Line had just reached Ruislip and a nucleus of 1,300 acres was owned by a highly sympathetic body (King's College, Cambridge). The paradigm planning achievement under the 1909 Act was the comparatively orderly metamorphosis of rural areas on the urban fringe into suburban developments which owed something, at least, to the garden city ideal.

Opposition to these achievements was largely on the grounds that such planning represented an ineffective compromise. Trystan Edwards continued to argue for New Towns on the ground that the existing suburban developments merely blurred the perfectly good distinction between town and country. C. B. Purdom suggested (in *Garden Cities and Town Planning* published in 1914) that the Garden City Movement had sold out to the Garden Suburb compromise.[1] The distinction between the compromise and the original ideal was to become more apparent in the inter-war period with increasing concern about the social consequences of the overall size of conurbations.

The Planning Act of 1919 was not intended to meet these radical criticisms. It made the construction of plans (that is, schemes for development) compulsory for local authorities with more than 20,000 population, simplified the process of their ministerial approval, and extended the possibility of central financial help to local authorities. The 1924 Housing Act is normally linked with the name of John Wheatley, the Roman Catholic, Independent Labour Party, 'Clydesider', who was Minister of Health in Ramsay MacDonald's first government. It incorporated two important and lasting principles of house construction. Authorities were empowered to construct houses which they themselves would own, paying by loan and recovering partially through rent; in other words, it created 'council houses'. Almost as important was that houses were to be built at a maximum density of twelve to the acre, thus implementing the recommendations of the Tudor Walters Committee, a Committee of the Local Government Board which had reported in 1918.

The 1929 Local Government Act included a putative broadening of the scope of the planning process by requiring county councils to be involved in negotiation and consultation about planning schemes and by empowering the Minister of Health to force the creation of joint, inter-authority, planning committees. The 1932 Town and Country Planning Act looked, on the face of it, as if it were going to take the process of broadening a great deal further. It allowed local authorities to prepare schemes for almost any kind of land (though control of agricultural building was, for instance, excluded). Comprehensive plans were to be drawn up within a three-year period and then approved by Parliament. But this process was too inflexible to allow real control. A developer could, in this period, apply for planning permission under the clauses covering 'interim development control'. The only sanction against his failing to do so, or ignoring refusal, was that he might, eventually, be required to undevelop. If this sanction were to be regularly applied, there would be private financial disasters without corresponding public benefits. For this reason, the 1932 Act was by no means so important as it looks as if it ought to have been. Nor was the Restriction of Ribbon Development Act of 1935, which was intended to control linear development along main roads through the machinery of the 1932 Act.

THE WORKING OF THE NEW MACHINERY

By 1942, 73 per cent of England and 36 per cent of Wales was subject to 'interim development control'. But only 5 per cent of land in England and 1 per cent in Wales was under a fully operative scheme. There were 1,4000 planning authorities, though in many cases they were linked by joint committees. Even so, giving planning powers to the lowest tier of local government posed insuperable problems. In the Manchester conurbation, for instance, eighty local authorities had planning powers within an area of 750 square miles. It is not difficult to imagine the diseconomies which could result if housing policy in (say) Stretford and Salford were not co-ordinated nor to infer that these were not economically nor administratively the natural units for planning.

In many ways, planning was more effective in the period 1909-19 than it was in the period 1919-39. This may seem odd, because the powers which planning authorities possessed were greater in the later period. But the machinery which was established in 1909 was established for, and had succeeded in, the controlling of new housing development so that it should be of a certain quality (low density, adequately equipped, related to road development, and so on). By the 1920s, these standards had become social and administrative norms; the planning machinery was scarcely needed to enforce them. One planner had written before 1914 that already local government officials, architects and builders were ashamed to be associated with any development which did not fall into the 'garden suburb' mould. So whereas the 1909-19 system had solved its problem (the nature and quality of residential development), the 1919-39 system did not prove effective in solving the new problems which had emerged: the overall balance of town and country, the co-ordination of industrial and residential development, and the consequences of the size of conurbations. The reasons for this failure are fairly clear. The planning machinery was too local; no initiatives were possible within it; its sanctions were clumsy. Worst of all, the authorities could not afford to pay compensation in cases where planning should have involved the prevention of development. As the Uthwatt Committee later pointed out, there were a number of constraints which caused local authorities to fight shy of preventative planning. Their local status vis-à-vis other local authorities, the fear of having to pay compensation, the political interest in increasing rateable value, the directly or indirectly expressed interests of local trade: these factors meant that it was a brave authority and a clear case before any effective prevention took place.

Thus 'planning' existed to confirm economic and social trends. The demarcation lines on maps in local government offices between industrial and residential zones made little difference to what happened. In any case, enough land had been scheduled for housing by 1939 to accommodate 350 million people at the Tudor Walters density. The system could build physically tolerable houses even if it did not always co-ordinate their building, in terms of their inhabitants' lives, with work, with leisure facilities or with transport. A clear case was the extension of London beyond Ilford into south-west Essex in the early 1920s; this took place without corresponding industrial development until the opening of the Ford plant at Dagenham in 1929. However, 2·7 million houses were built between 1930 and 1939, so that by the war one-third of all existing houses had been built since 1912. Greater London had expanded by 2 million people; it was in this period that Middlesex was almost entirely urbanised by development which was quite new in human experience in its rapidity and uniformity.

By 1939 the problems of the nineteenth century had largely been solved; the proletariat was relatively healthy, orderly and stable. But the solutions to these problems were themselves problems. The new problems were less immediate and less clearly problems, but they were on a much larger scale than the old ones. I intend to examine three of them: the overall size of urban areas; the distribution of the industrial population; and the decline of agriculture.

THE SIZE OF URBAN AREAS

The Scott Committee[2] recorded that England and Wales (the unit for legislation) was by 1939 the most densely populated country in the world. It had 703 people per square mile as compared with 702 for Belgium, 633 for Holland and under 400 for every other country. The breakdown of land use in England and Wales, according to the Committee's interpretation of the figures produced by the Land Utilisation Survey, was:

82·1% in agricultural production;
 1·1% other open land;
 5·5% woodland;
11·3% 'in buildings, roads and other forms of constructional development, or otherwise unaccounted for in agricultural returns'.

This last figure does not constitute a figure for urban area. The more reliable figures provided by Best and Coppock[3] over twenty years later show a slightly lower figure for urban areas so we can be certain that this figure, calculated as a residue, is a considerable overestimate. Even so, the rate of urbanisation was staggering. In the twelve years before 1939 the urbanisation of rural land proceeded at 66,200 acres a year. Scott estimated that 10 per cent could be subtracted from this as 'returnable' (largely military) development, so that a more 'real' figure would be 60,000 acres. This represented well over 2 per cent of the entire area of England changing from rural to urban in a twelve-year period. That is, there was twice the average annual rate of urbanisation that there has been since 1945. One can only guess at the percentage increase in the whole urban area between 1918 and 1939, but the figure of 50 per cent to 60 per cent seems reasonable. Ten thousand years of civilisation (in the literal sense) halved again in twenty-one years!

This progress worried those who concerned themselves with planning in a number of ways. Firstly, there was concern about the consequent loss of agricultural production. This fear did not persist after the Second World War, partly because increased agricultural efficiency allowed Britain to increase her proportion of home-produced food and partly because it was shown during the war that efficient gardening in housing areas with Tudor Walters densities could produce an amount of food only marginally less than the normal agricultural production for the same land. A more lasting concern, which I will examine later, was with the loss of beauty and of space; it has always been difficult to assess the importance of such loss, but it certainly caused a great deal of concern to the Scott and Dower Committees.

Most immediately, the increasing size of the conurbations was beginning to have a marked effect on the economy of cities and the quality of life within cities. Early planning had established strong arguments for having separate industrial and residential zones in an urban area, so that people did not have to live too closely with noise and pollution. But the separation was becoming too great; in London, in particular, people were being faced with a choice between (in the words of one speaker at the Oxford Planning Conference of 1941) 'straphanging and the tenement'.[4] As early as 1930, the President of the Commercial Motor Users Association had estimated that for people working within a three-mile radius of Charing Cross travelling time was equivalent to one-eighth of working time. Now it was the very size, not the condition, of London which posed the problem and the form in which ordinary citizens encountered the problem was the journey to work.

THE DISTRIBUTION OF THE INDUSTRIAL POPULATION

Between 1923 and 1934 the number of insured workers in south-eastern England rose by 44 per cent. In the same period, the number of workers in the north-east fell by 5·5 per cent and the number in Wales by 2·6 per cent. The economic crisis exacerbated the effects of the decline of primary and 'heavy' industry with the result that unemployment in some towns in northern England remained at 20 or 30 per cent over a long period. At the same time, a majority in the south enjoyed a standard of living which was high by historical or international standards. The Special Areas Act of 1934 created Industrial Commissions for England and Wales and for Scotland in an attempt to alleviate the problems of the areas of high unemployment, but its effect was only marginal. These economic forces, and the process of urbanisation, thus reinforced each other as problems; as a result, town and country planning again entered the mainstream of political issues.

The Barlow Commission's report[5] was the keystone of future planning, economic and environmental; it outlined the broad, general strategies and methods within which planning would work. The Commission had been appointed to inquire into 'the present geographical distribution of the industrial population of Great Britain . . . its social, economic or strategic disadvantages . . . remedial measures if any. . . .' It reported in 1940. It concluded that there should be national action, in the hands of a 'Central Authority' whose powers went beyond those of any existing body. The Authority should act to disperse industry throughout the whole country and diversify it within particular regions. Especially, it should try to control the further growth of London. Planning should be on a regional, rather than a municipal, scale and should involve the creation of new cities, towns and suburbs. The Central Authority should have general control of all planning machinery and should collect information on all matters related to planning. This would include economic and industrial information as well as information about natural resources and amenities. Naturally, this information was to be influential in the creation of general strategies for planning.

THE DECLINE OF AGRICULTURE

The Scott Committee concerned itself with rural decline in two senses. Firstly, in the decline of agriculture as an industry. Secondly, in the decline of the countryside both in total area and in aesthetic beauty.

The decline of British agriculture, which had begun in the 1870s, had only been temporarily arrested by the economic situation in the Great War. During the inter-war period it continued rapidly. Whereas there had been an average of 816,000 workers in agriculture in the period 1921-4, there were only 539,000 by 1938: a 25 per cent decline. The number of male workers under 21 had dropped by 44 per cent in the same period.

Scott claimed that this process had created an air of depression over the countryside. The drift to the towns often involved individual 'choices' which were regretted and regrettable, but which were made inevitable by the financial situation in which agricultural workers found themselves. One common factor was the inability of young agricultural workers to rent cottages, especially when there were industrial competitors for the same accommodation. By June 1939, the average weekly wage for agricultural labour varied from £1 12s 0d to £1 17s 6d. This had only risen from between £1 7s 0d and £1 12s 0d since 1923. In 1939 the average industrial wage for unskilled workers varied between £2 3s 0d and £3 0s 0d. Only 30,000 of 365,972 agricultural holdings were equipped with electricity. Of the 7 million people who lived in communities of under 1,500, about 1 million were without piped water.

The Scott Report recommended the provision of subsidised housing for agricultural labour, the provision of agricultural subsidies and the provision of state schemes to facilitate capital-formation in agriculture. Water and electricity were to be provided at costs which did not discriminate against the agricultural areas, however remote. More generally, the report recommended the inclusion of all rural areas in planning schemes. This implied the control of agricultural building (specifically excluded in the 1932 Act) and the effective 'zoning' of some land as not being available for development. To this end, it was recommended that central government should be able to compel the formation of joint planning committees and that planning authorities should not have to pay compensation for loss of development rights on agricultural land. Planning was to be based on counties and county boroughs normally under the supervision of a Central Planning Commission which would, in turn, be controlled by an integrated structure of the relevant ministries. Because local authorities were to be used, in effect, for the implementation of national plans, they were to be given financial assistance by the central government for planning and its consequences. In the report it was recommended, for the first time, that planning authorities should be required to employ 'qualified personnel'. The report recommended not only this framework and set of procedures, but also certain policies which should be pursued within them. These included the provision of National Parks and Nature Reserves, the classification of footpaths and the elimination of some unsightly objects (such as garages and advertisements) from the countryside.

THE NEW PLANNING ISSUES

By 1939 there was broad consensus amongst the administrators, intellectuals and businessmen who concerned themselves with planning that radical change was necessary—just as there had been in the years before 1909. Evidence of this broadly based desire for change comes from many sources, but I will concentrate on the discussions of the Oxford Planning Conference of March 1941.[6] The vast majority of writers on planning and practitioners of planning were present, as well as many other academics and administrators. John Dower, Sir Montague Barlow and Lord Justice Scott were all there. So were D. N. Chester, G. D. H. Cole, Sir Richard Ensor, Lord Harmsworth, Professor Holford, F. J. Osborn, W. A. Robson, Lord Samuel, Lewis Silkin, Dudley Stamp, Sir Ernest Simon and two members of the Cadbury family. All were, or were about to become, distinguished in the fields of administration, business, politics or the universities. In short, it was as comprehensive a selection of the administrative intellects of the time as one could hope to find. This was the first major conference after the publication of the Barlow Report and invitations to it said that it would be assumed that all those who chose to attend would be 'in agreement with the principles unanimously accepted by the Royal Commission'[7] so that discussion could take place within those premises. But although everyone accepted these principles, there remained a number of ambiguities and strategic dilemmas which divided delegates sharply.

One of these concerned the role of New Towns in future planning. The idea of specially constructing New Towns as a cure for social problems was a very old one and had, of course, been part of Ebenezer Howard's programme. The idea had slipped into the background in the years immediately after 1909, but it had returned to the debate as planners concentrated their attentions on problems of a larger scale. Trystan Edwards had been a consistent advocate of a New Towns' policy; his advocacy had included a book, *One Hundred New Towns for Britain*, which was supported by a wide range of planners in a letter to *The Times* in 1933. Controversy existed about the importance of New Towns in future planning policy and about what New Towns would be like. At the Oxford Conference, for instance, F. J. Osborn suggested that it was possible and desirable to 'decentralise' about 5 million people to 'satellite' towns. He calculated that if densities of twenty or twenty-five habitations to the acre were allowed, only half a million acres of agricultural land would be needed ($1 \cdot 5$ per cent of the total). On the other hand, Lewis Silkin for the London County Council argued that thinking about New Towns was on a dubiously impractical level. He claimed that London could substantially solve its own problems by the construction of flats at up to sixty habitations per acre. Where possible, flats should be provided at thirty to the acre which could 'make very good homes with all modern amenities'. E. H. Ford, the City Engineer and Surveyor of Coventry, expressed the hope that the idea of the garden city would not lose its impetus. He did not want to see high density flats built in existing urban areas. His colleague, D. E. E. Gibson, the City Architect of Coventry, also defended low-density principles but Herbert Manzoni, Birmingham's Chief Engineer and Surveyor, suggested that their application had been 'too slavish'.

There were differences of interpretation of the idea of a 'Central Authority'. Abercrombie suggested what was, in effect, a Department of the Environment—he called it a 'suzerain ministry'. It was to have powers over other ministries and to co-ordinate all land planning. Others were divided as to whether the 'Central Authority' should be a ministry and, if it should, what sort of ministry it should be. There were also a variety of ideas about the form of the more local administration. Regional boards, county councils and county boroughs, and joint planning committees were all mooted as potential institutions for the possession of local planning powers.

Ideas about regional planning were commonly expressed but remained, on the whole, extremely vague. There had been since 1927 a Greater London Regional Planning Committee and since 1931 a Ministry of Health Committee on regional planning, but little thought had been given to the practical problems of integrating regional structures.

Finally, there was the oldest problem of all planning: the concept of property and its interpretation. Everybody agreed that future planning could not be constrained by having to pay 'full' compensation for loss of development rights in every case. How this could be avoided was more derisive. By compulsory 'pooling' of land ownership? By nationalisation of all land? By acquiring the freehold of all land? By assuming development rights belonged to the state, though the land belonged to the owner? By paying compensation only on 'original use' values? All these were suggested.

The Uthwatt Committee recommended that betterment should be collected (75 per cent of the increase in value), and compensation paid, on a notion of 'site value'. This 'site value' should be assessed quinquennially by the rating valuers and should be based on the assumption that the land was permanently restricted to its present use. Up to 4 per cent of betterment could be allowed for actual cash expenditure by the owner. Thus, in an English compromise, the idea of separating the attributes of ownership and control became established. It has been crucial to British planning ever since.

THE IMPACT OF THE SECOND WORLD WAR

Some writers consider that the main effect of war was its physical destruction which opened the possibility of reconstructing city centres wholesale as nothing else could have done.[8] Plymouth and Coventry are the clearest examples. But the most important effect of the war was on the administrative imagination: normally cautious men expressed radical ideas as if they were undeniable. Planning became accepted as a word and as an idea at every level; this involved the rejection of traditional ideas of economic and financial 'necessity'. The intellectual rejection of these ideas had been taking place before the war, particularly with the publication of Maynard Keynes' *General Theory*[9] in 1936. But the war rapidly accelerated the acceptance of the new ideas. This emerges from the debate on land ownership at the Oxford Conference. Both the major speakers, Sir Ernest Simon and John Eccles, proposed the nationalisation of land. In the informal discussion, Sir Henry Lawrence cited Hitler as having demonstrated the fallacy of economic laws and financial constraints. 'Germany thought in terms of manpower and materials instead of being limited by lack of money',[10] he said. Thus the success of the German war machine. He quoted Keynes's expression: 'the humbug of finance'.

By 1945, to judge from the speeches, letters and leaders in *The Times* pertaining to the election, it was virtually an orthodoxy to believe that unemployment had been caused by a false economic theory which Lord Keynes had now kindly exposed, and by the typical timidity of the

D

appeasement politicians. The future lay with state planning; it was almost as if financial problems and economic laws had disappeared in a whiff of Keynesian bleach. It did not seem to occur to many people that war was a special situation which required (and allowed) methods which could not work in peace-time.

This change of ideas was an over-reaction. I agree with Ashworth that one consequence of winning the war was 'a somewhat unreflecting public desire that similar processes should be continued in peace-time for different objects, in the hope that equally spectacular successes would be achieved'.[11] The positive side of this was that a basis of future policy had been agreed by planners and administrators and that the values and theories which would have militated against this basis in the thirties had been severely weakened where they had not been destroyed.

THE POET AS PLANNER: ARTISTIC REACTIONS TO URBANISATION

The massive urbanisation of the inter-war period was not a private problem for the administrative intellects who assembled in Oxford in March 1941. It had aroused fearful and concerned responses from a much wider section of the community. As early as 1913, Trystan Edwards had commented, 'Even the poor cannot live by bread alone', implying that there was something missing in the much-vaunted housing developments of the period. I have already quoted the reactions expressed by D. H. Lawrence in his 1929 essay, 'Nottingham and the Mining Countryside'.

The development of large areas of hygienically satisfactory, but aesthetically unsatisfying, cheap housing, provoked a sharp reaction from a wide variety of contemporaries. Here is an example of a description by Evelyn Waugh of the English landscape at the end of the twenties:

'Ginger looked out of the aeroplane: "I say, Nina," he shouted, "when you were young did you ever have to learn a thing out of a poetry book about 'This scepter'd isle, this earth of majesty, this something or other Eden?' D'you know what I mean? 'this happy breed of men, this precious stone set in the silver sea . . .

> This blessed plot, this earth, this realm, this England
> This nurse, this teeming womb of royal kings
> Feared by their breed and famous by their birth . . .'

Well I mean to say, don't you feel somehow, up in the air like this and looking down and seeing everything underneath. I mean, don't you have a sort of feeling rather like that, if you see what I mean?"

'Nina looked down and saw inclined at an odd angle an horizon of straggling red suburb; arterial roads dotted with little cars; factories, some of them working, others empty and decayed; a disused canal; some distant hills sown with bungalows; wireless masts and overhead cables; men and women were indiscernible except as tiny spots; they were marrying and shopping and making money and having children. The scene lurched and tilted again as the aeroplane struck a current of air. ' "I think I'm going to be sick," said Nina.'[12]

This mediocrity, social change which threatened to culminate in ugliness and uniformity, obsessed George Orwell, particularly in his last pre-war novel, *Coming up for Air*. The leading character, George Bowling, is an ex-grocer's assistant who has known a kind of glory as an army officer in the Great War but who now, at the age of 45, ekes out his life as a traveller in insurance. Early in the book he describes the area he lives in:

'Do you know the road I live in—Ellesmere Road, West Bletchley? Even if you don't, you know fifty others exactly like it.

'You know how these streets fester all over the inner-outer suburbs. Always the same. Long, long rows of little semi-detached houses—the numbers in Ellesmere Road run to 212 and ours is 191—as much alike as council houses and generally uglier. The stucco front, the creosoted gate, the privet hedge, the green front door. The Laurels, the Myrtles, the Hawthorns, Mon Abri, Mon Repos, Belle Vue. At perhaps one house in fifty some anti-social type who'll probably end in the work-house has painted his front door blue instead of green.'[13]

A more effective passage, foreshadowing a great deal of 1984 in its sheer distaste for life, is directed against mass-produced food:

'The frankfurter had a rubber skin, of course, and my temporary teeth weren't much of a fit. I had to do a kind of sawing movement before I could get my teeth through the skin, and then suddenly—pop! The thing burst in my mouth like a rotten pear. A sort of horrible soft stuff was oozing all over my tongue. But the taste! For a moment I just couldn't believe it. Then I rolled my tongue round it again and had another try. It was *fish*! A sausage, a thing calling itself a frankfurter, filled with fish! I got up and walked straight out without touching my coffee. God knows what that might have tasted of.'[14]

In the fourth and last part of *Coming up for Air*, George Bowling returns, ostensibly for some fishing, to his home village of Lower Binfield, after an absence of fifteen years. This allows Orwell to devote more specific attention to the state of the English landscape:

'I rounded the bend and came in sight of the towpath. Christ! Another jolt. The place was black with people. And where the water-meadows used to be—tea-houses, penny-in-the-slot machines, sweet kiosks and chaps selling Walls' Ice Cream. Might as well have been at Margate. I remember the old towpath. You could walk along it for miles, and except for the chaps at the local gates, and now and again a bargeman mooching along behind his horse, you'd never meet a soul.'[15]

It is the privilege of the *literateur*, as opposed to the planner or the politician, to be allowed to reject all possible alternatives. Orwell felt strongly repugnant both towards the working-class poverty which he found in Lancashire (and described in *The Road to Wigan Pier*) and towards the working-class prosperity he observed in the south-east in the late thirties. Lawrence was more consistent in that he had in mind a real way of life which was preferable: the mining villages of his father's generation. These three writers—Lawrence, Waugh and Orwell—are associated with totally different political positions. None of them concerned himself directly with the physical landscape. Orwell's prime target (or fear) was totalitarianism, Waugh's was egalitarianism or the decline of style, Lawrence's was emasculation. But to all three the physical state of England both symbolised, and was part of, the deeper situation. The ugliness, the mediocrity, the frightening expansion of urban and suburban areas, were the outward and visible signs of some deep-seated change for the worse.

Nor were these three isolated examples. Indeed, it would be difficult to draw up a list of 'intellectuals' of any eminence in the thirties who were not concerned with the physical state of the English landscape. An imposing list of those who were concerned can be found in a set of essays edited by Clough Williams-Ellis under the title *Britain and the Beast*[16] which was published in 1938. The 'Beast' in question is industrial urbanisation and the essays in the book are all concerned with the nature and implications of the threat to the countryside and the possible means of its salvation. Messages of support for the publication of the book were received from Lloyd George, Sir Kingsley Wood (Minister of Health), George Lansbury, Lord Baden-Powell, Sir Stafford Cripps, Julian Huxley and J. B. Priestley. In one essay, E. M. Forster referred to 'the England which we love and are losing',[17] and that phrase encapsulates the assumptions of almost all the contributors. J. M. Keynes wrote of the relationship between the state and the quality of life. Forster attacked the armed forces for their mistreatment of the countryside. C. E. M. Joad, the Oxford philosopher, wrote of the need for educating the masses to the enjoyment and proper use of the countryside. G. M. Trevelyan summed up the prescriptive conclusion in arguing that: 'In the matter of the preservation of the beauty of rural England, what we need is a State policy, the support of the Ministry, of Parliament and of legislation.'[18] Thomas Sharp and

Patrick Abercrombie wrote essays on the nature and possibility of rural planning and the prevention of ugly urbanisation. The idea of rural planning owed a great deal to Abercrombie. His essay, 'The Preservation of Rural England',[19] had provided the immediate rationale of the foundation of the Council for the Preservation of Rural England in 1926. His important textbook,[20] published in 1933, devoted one-third of its content to rural planning and specified the important distinction between a policy for 'wild' country and a policy for 'tame' country. Rural planning really became established in the war. The situation is exemplified by a remark made by Mr B. Bell, Planning Officer of Kesteven Joint Planning Committee, to the Town and Country Planning Association's conference of December 1944:

'Sir Arthur [Hobhouse] made an important statement when he said that every planning officer should have had some experience in rural planning. I entirely agree, and should like to give an example. Fifteen years ago I was a student at one of the two big planning schools in this country and in those two years, not one single lecture was given in which the problems of rural planning were discussed.'[21]

This campaign for the countryside can be accused of a number of political sins. It was certainly élitist in its membership and sometimes (very clearly in Joad's case) in its paternalistic attitudes. There was an element of hypocrisy in the way that many writers blithely and vaguely blamed 'industrialism' for destroying the countryside when higher standards of housing were the main factor behind urbanisation. There was also a great deal of rationalisation in that what was, for most people, an emotional and personal love of the English countryside, was argued in terms of benefits to the masses.

Nevertheless, it was an impressive and effective movement. It produced recommendations for the preservation of the countryside and for the inclusion of a greater aesthetic dimension in planning which were largely implemented after 1945. It was supported by fine minds, the alliance of which cut across all normal ideological and political divisions. Its impact is still visible.

NOTES

1. In Purdom's book published in the same year (C. B. Purdom, *The Garden City: A Study in the Development of a Modern Town* (London, Dent, 1913)) he insisted that: 'Town planning on Garden City lines is the planning of new small towns. It is nothing else. The fact that the new suburbs appropriate part of the name of the new town, and even allow themselves to imitate certain details of its development is, perhaps, a compliment to the Garden City, but it is nothing more' (Purdom, op. cit., p. 203).

2. *Land Utilisation in Rural Areas,* Committee on (Chairman, the Right Honourable Lord Justice Scott, PC), Cmd. 6378 (London, HMSO, 1942).
3. R. H. Best and J. T. Coppock, *The Changing Use of Land in Britain* (London, Faber, 1962).
4. F. E. Towndrow (ed.), *Replanning Britain,* being a summarised report of the Oxford Conference of the Town and Country Planning Association, Spring 1941 (London, Faber, 1941), p. 111.
5. *Report of the Royal Commission on the Distribution of the Industrial Population* (Chairman, the Right Honourable Sir Montague Barlow, KBE, LLD), Cmd. 6153 (London, HMSO, 1940).
6. Towndrow, op. cit.
7. Ibid., p. 11.
8. See, for example, E. C. Hargrove, 'Tradition and Change in England', in *Comparative Politics,* Vol. 4, No. 4 (1972).
9. J. M. Keynes, *The General Theory of Employment, Interest and Money* (London, Macmillan, 1936).
10. Towndrow, op. cit., pp. 133-4.
11. William Ashworth, *The Genesis of Modern British Town Planning* (London, Routledge, 1954), pp. 230-1.
12. Evelyn Waugh, *Vile Bodies* (1930; London, Chapman and Hall, 1965), pp. 196-7.
13. George Orwell, *Coming up for Air* (1939; Secker and Warburg, 1963), p. 13.
14. Ibid., p. 27.
15. Ibid., p. 204.
16. Clough Williams-Ellis (ed.), *Britain and the Beast* (Readers' Union by arrangement with J. M. Dent, 1938). Not to be confused with the Moral Rearmament tract of the same name.
17. Ibid., p. 44.
18. Ibid., p. 183.
19. In *Journal of the Town Planning Institute* (1926).
20. Patrick Abercrombie, *Town and Country Planning* (Oxford, OUP, 1933), Part 3.
21. Barbara Bliss (ed.), *The New Planning,* report of the TCPA Conference of December 1944 (London, Faber, 1944), p. 98.

Chapter 5

1947 and All That

The Town and Country Planning Act of 1947 'embodied the principle that all development rights belonged to the state'.[1] It created machinery for comprehensive planning of all land in England and Wales; there was parallel legislation for Scotland. During the subsequent twenty years that machinery was modified and codified by a number of legislative Acts but it remained substantially as it had been established in 1947.[2] It is the purpose of this chapter to describe the core of that machinery[3] as a set of political institutions with only a minimum of moral and sociological comment.

'Planning' in the expressions 'town planning', 'town and country planning' and 'environmental planning' can mean a number of distinct activities (as well as combinations of them):

1. In an ideal world, a system in which everything which happens is a publicly chosen alternative.
2. Co-ordinating actions which would not otherwise be co-ordinated in terms of stated objectives.
3. It can mean simply that private and organisational actions are subjected to public control (without necessarily any clear objectives).
4. Projecting future trends and contingencies in the light of which policy can be made. In this sense, planning is an aid to the making of decisions rather than decision-making itself.
5. Projection allied to a choice between strategies, taking some factors as given and others as open to choice.

'Planning' in the United States has been largely of type-4, but in Britain it has consisted of both type-3 and type-5. The system created in 1947 obliged planning authorities to draw up 'development plans', a combination of strategy and projection covering a period of twenty years. Development plans consisted of a written statement and a number of maps. Between them these expressed intentions for development and intentions for preservation in different areas under the planning authority's control. Many plans for rural areas contained, for instance, a classification of villages into 'A', 'B', 'C' and 'D' or '1', '2', '3' and '4', indicating villages where no development should be allowed, those where 'infilling' development might be allowed, those where suitable expansion should be allowed, and those where, for some reason, major expansion was to take place. Some land was left as 'white area' in which it was assumed (though not necessarily firmly intended) that the existing land use would continue. Plans were the responsibility of local planning authorities—primarily of the 'biggest' units, the counties and county boroughs. They were actually created by planning departments, professional and expert administrations which the authorities were obliged to employ, and submitted by the authority to the minister who could accept them, reject them, or (more likely) require their modification. Development plans had to be revised every five years. The name of the ministry responsible for planning has, incidentally, changed twice; from 1947 to 1951 it was the Ministry of Town and Country Planning and from 1951 to 1970 the Ministry of Housing and Local Government before becoming the Department of the Environment in 1970.

Individuals and organisations were directly affected by this system in that they required planning permission for any development, though there turned out to be (perhaps inevitably) a number of loop-holes in this requirement. Certain types of development did not require any permission at all; these were classified under the Use Classes Order and the General Development Order and they included 'similar' uses and house extensions of 10 per cent and under in any one year. A local authority could require a development project exempted from the need for permission to submit its plans and it could still then refuse permission, but if it did it would be required to pay compensation in full. Failure to submit plans not exempt, or developing despite a refusal of planning permission, could be followed by an enforcement order requiring the developer to undevelop. Failure to comply with such an order could result in a fine or imprisonment.

For large projects, planning permission could be divided into two halves, 'outline' and 'detailed' permission, in order that architectural effort (and clients' money) should not be wasted on detailed plans for a non-starter. Applications for detailed planning permission should be made within two years of receiving outline permission. This did not mean that detailed planning permission would be given then; in one case there was a period of fourteen years between the granting of outline permission and the granting of detailed permission. It was certainly not generally believed that dividing an application into two made it any easier to obtain final permission.

Anyone who was refused planning permission by a local authority could appeal to the minister. This could be done in two ways: either by purely written representations or by requiring the minister to hold a public local inquiry. At such inquiries an inspector from the ministry heard the case put by the developer and any objections to the development which other individuals or organisations might wish to put. Then he wrote a report to the minister who finally refused or allowed permission.

The total number of planning applications remained remarkably constant. It was just over 400,000 in both 1958 and 1969. Approximately 85 per cent of applications were granted in 1969, 90 per cent in 1958. In 1958 about 20 per cent of refusals were appealed and just under one-third of these were granted. This looks like a very high proportion of decisions being reversed; the usual explanation of this is that it was the best cases (normally advised and presented by professional lawyers) which were appealed.

There is a constitutional fiction associated with the idea of 'the minister'. No minister could possibly consider the number of inspectors' reports which the minister is said to have received. In the 1960s the number of public inquiries arising from both public proposals and private proposals through the local government machinery was some-times over 10,000 a year. In fact, the conclusions of inspectors' reports were accepted in over 95 per cent of cases. There were about 150 inspectors in the central core of the planning inspectorate. These were mainly full-time civil servants, but sometimes retired civil servants or even outsiders. A retired army officer presided over the largest inquiry which has been held in Britain so far. Within the ministry, a 'decisions group' of Administrative Grade officials processed inspectors' reports. Very few decisions would involve a minister in anything more than a rubber-stamp capacity. There would be ones which seemed potentially or actually controversial or important for future policy. Crudely, civil servants would give decisions to ministers if they were afraid of making the commitment themselves. Similarly, ministers would present decisions to Cabinet if they felt that it would be improper (or dangerous) to take personal responsibilities for them. In the mid-1960s decisions on the proposal to have a road through Christ Church Meadow, Oxford, and on the Manchester Water Order on Ullswater and Windermere and possibly others were discussed at Cabinet level.

It is an over-simplification to suppose that the development plan once approved—normally after a public inquiry—furnished hard and fast criteria for dealing with applications for planning permission. The rela-tionship was much looser than that; it has been officially described thus:

'The development plan is . . . only a broad strategic framework; it does not go into precise detail or show exactly what development will, or will not, be allowed. If proposals for development do not accord with the plan, the local authority can give its consent if it believes that they do not involve a substantial departure from the plan or affect the whole of the neighbourhood.'⁴

In any case, it was often necessary for planning authorities to make decisions without a plan or with only a plan in need of review. The local authority could also allow permission for developments which were important and did not appear compatible with the plan, provided that it lodged a copy of the application with the minister and gave public notice of its intention, allowing representations from any person or body who objected. But for many cases there did seem to be an asymmetry between citizens in their relation to the planning system: developers had the right to appeal against any refusal of permission, but those who opposed a development had no equivalent right in the event of permission being granted, unless they were invited to make representations for a specific reason (an appeal against a refusal or clear incompatibility with the plan, for instance). This inequity was worsened by the difficulty of providing public information about planning applications. Any citizen had the right to examine the planning register—though it seems doubtful whether more than a very small percentage would have known where the planning office was—and more important issues required public site notices. In practice, the amenity societies and the local press were admitted to be the effective means of communication with the public.

It is important to realise the constraints which central government effectively put on the planning decisions of local authorities. In the first place, central government approval was needed for all plans and all specific designations such as green belts. Then individual refusals could be appealed to central government. The legislative and administrative policies of the centre virtually decided planning policy in advance for some areas; there was little point for a local authority in trying to encourage development in an area designated as a National Park or Area of Outstanding Natural Beauty or in trying to prevent development in a centrally designated development area or New Town area. If a local authority allowed permission which central government did not want, the application could be 'called in' for direct administration by the ministry. In such a case, if permission was then refused, the local authority had to pay full compensation to the developer. The calling-in procedure was rarely used but it was an effective 'Damocles' sword' hanging over the head of any local authority which wished to be defiant of ministry policies.

This relationship of control affected the internal working of local government, for it made the role of the professional even more important than it would otherwise have been. Only the professionals really understood planning and the implications of their plans for planning applications. It was difficult where not impossible for an elected councillor to challenge a plan even if he had sufficient expertise, which was unlikely. In order to seriously effect the plan he would have had to spend a great deal of time on it; in effect to do the professional's job for him. It has been estimated that 70 per cent of planning applications were dealt with entirely by planning officials; apparently planning committees took an average of only two to three minutes to deal with an application. Add these factors to the situation in which local planning officials could pose, too, as the interpreters of national policy and its criteria, and one can come to understand the description of one planning officer of what happened when there was conflict between his chief and the council: 'Oh, Mr X [the Chief Planning Officer] just has a word with them and then does what he thinks is right.' This relationship may not have been entirely typical, but it was certainly possible.

The relationship between councils and their planning committees was also the reverse of what democracy would require. Councils became the rubber stamp mechanisms for committee decisions. The relationship certainly worked both ways in that councillors on planning committees represented their fellow-councillors' opinions to the planners and the planners' problems and decisions to their colleagues on the council. But it was commonly observed that members of planning committees often developed a close rapport with planners and came to consider planning criteria as being 'above' party politics. An interesting example of this reaction is related by Gregory in his description of the Holme Pierrepoint power station controversy of 1960-3.[5] A power station had to be built somewhere in the Nottingham area. It was a central government decision as to where it should be built, but the local authorities' recommendations would be important in determining the site. Holme Pierrepoint was generally agreed to be the best site, particularly in relation to transport facilities. Both the National Union of Mineworkers and the local business community were in favour of Holme Pierrepoint. But the local authorities (Nottingham County Council and Nottingham City Council) recommended that it be not built. This was particularly strange in the case of Nottingham County Council which contained a majority of miners and miners' wives. They did so on the recommendation of their own planning committee which argued that Holme Pierrepoint was in a proposed green belt and that, therefore, the power station would be indefensible on planning grounds. So the administrative criteria of the planning system over-rode local economic interests; in the end the power station was not built at Holme Pierrepoint, but at Ratcliffe-on-Soar, nine miles south of Nottingham.

By locating planning functions at the biggest level of local government, the 1947 Act cured some of the discord in relationship between different authorities which had existed in the inter-war period. But it was still necessary for authorities to co-ordinate their policies. There were two kinds of relationship. Firstly, the relationship between authorities of equal stature. By the 1960s it was necessary, for instance, for Warwickshire to co-ordinate its plans with those of Coventry and Solihull through the Coventry-Solihull-Warwickshire sub-regional survey which fully employed officials of all three authorities. This in turn had to work with reference to the West Midlands regional plan in the regional economic planning structure set up under the Labour Government's Department of Economic Affairs. It was also necessary for joint committees of local authorities to manage the National Parks; the Lake District was the most complex, requiring co-ordination between Cumberland, Westmorland and Lancashire. Secondly, there were the hierarchical relationships between counties and the smaller authorities within them—rural districts, urban districts and non-county boroughs. There are obvious economies and efficiencies in having these levels deal with their own problems so far as that is compatible with overall plans. The 1947 Act allowed for such delegation and the possibility was interpreted in a wide variety of ways: sometimes a great deal of delegation, sometimes none at all; sometimes a stage in all relevant decisions, sometimes virtually complete control over certain categories of decision. After the Local Government Act of 1958, however, lower-tier authorities with a population of over 60,000 could require counties to delegate a wide variety of decisions to them, although they were still subject to the overall control of the counties.

Finally, I should make it clear that the planning structures I have described, the complex hierarchy of local authorities and the ministry, was not the only planning machinery. Many of the most important and noticeable developments were public projects and thus fell outside of the direct control of the local authorities and the Ministry of Housing and Local Government. Trunk roads were the responsibility of the Ministry of Transport and its road construction units, but local authorities were involved in their planning to furnish both opinion and information. Similarly, the coal, gas and electricity industries were the responsibility of public corporations under the Minister of Power, but they too became (often reluctantly) more integrated with the main structure of land-use planning. In general, there was a tendency over time for a greater integration between the main structure of land-use planning and the public use of land for transport and energy provision. The tendency culminated in the creation of the Department of the Environment in 1970.

THE PLANNING PROCESS AS POLICY-MAKER

Although the planning machinery was directed by national objectives and was increasingly integrated, these objectives were unclear and even conflicted in some cases. Economic development areas overlapped with National Parks; New Towns were designated on the edge of Areas of Outstanding Natural Beauty. Gregory quite rightly describes the process as 'piecemeal'; he stresses that there was no secret national master plan in Whitehall which decided whether plans were approved or appeals upheld. There was, however, an assortment of policies which amounted to a rough and ready national plan. In the matter of conservation, for instance, one estimate[6] had it that over 40 per cent of the total land surface was publicly protected. This included National Parks, Areas of Outstanding Natural Beauty, Crown Lands (such as the New Forest), National Trust properties, Forestry Commission Forest Parks, Nature Reserves, Sites of Special Scientific Interest, as well as areas proposed by local authorities as green belts or classified by them as Areas of Great Landscape Value. It probably did not include other land effectively, but less publicly, preserved by the policies incorporated in development plans. Even less tangibly, the criterion of 'amenity' (although vague to the point of meaninglessness) was a prevailing value in the planning system and 'having regard to the interests of amenity' was the duty of a number of public bodies—a duty first incorporated in statute in the Hydro-Electric Power (Scotland) Act of 1943.[7]

I have concentrated on conservation policies but, in the same way, strategies for development were loosely constructed and integrated within the system. The whole system can only be understood in terms of the British political culture and constitution. Basically, it was a system in which the legal fiction of 'the minister' responsible to Queen-in-Parliament allowed a considerable control by the bureaucracy of private uses of land, the control being exercised in terms of a number of ill-defined, though effective, values.

NOTES

1. Central Office of Information, *Town and Country Planning in Britain*, Reference Pamphlet 9 (London, HMSO, 1972), p. 9.
2. The main legislation includes: Town and Country Planning Acts 1947 (C. 51), 1947 (Scotland) (C. 53), 1962 (C. 38), 1962 (Scotland) (C. 38), 1963 (C. 17). Local Government (Miscellaneous Provisions) Act 1953 (C. 26); Local Authorities (Land) Act 1963 (C. 29); Compulsory Purchase Act 1965 (C. 56); Local Government Act 1966 (C. 42), Local Government (Scotland) Act 1966 (C. 51); Civic Amenities Act 1967 (C. 69); Countryside Act 1968 (C. 41).
3. The established textbook on planning is J. B. Cullingworth, *Town and Country Planning in England and Wales: An Introduction* (London,

Allen & Unwin, 1964) 1st edn. Desmond Heap, *An Outline of Planning Law* (London, Sweet & Maxwell, 1949), 1st edn, is an introduction to the legal aspects of planning. D. R. Mandelker, *Green Belts and Urban Growth: English Town and Country Planning in Action* (University of Wisconsin Press, 1962), is a simpler account from an American perspective. Brief accounts of the system are to be found in successive editions of Central Office of Information pamphlets (op. cit.) and in Robert Arvill, *Man and Environment* (Harmondsworth, Penguin, 1967). Roy Gregory, *The Price of Amenity* (London, Macmillan, 1971), offers through its case studies a sample of the administrative complexities of the system. I have used these works in constructing my account as well as newspaper, magazine and journal articles and numerous conversations with planners and academics interested in planning. I should especially like to express my gratitude to J. P. W. B. McAuslan, Professor of Law at the University of Warwick and Councillor of the Royal Borough of Leamington Spa. Needless to say, however, the impressions and opinions in this chapter are entirely my own responsibility.

4. Central Office of Information, op. cit., p. 8.
5. Gregory, op. cit., pp. 89-132.
6. *Report from the Select Committee on Nationalised Industries (The Electricity Supply Industry)* HC 236-1 (1962-3), 157. Quoted in Gregory, op. cit., p. 12.
7. The 'amenity clause' duty was extended to all public bodies in the Town and Country Planning Act of 1968. For a discussion of 'amenity' see Cullingworth, op. cit., pp. 132-56.

Chapter 6

Environmental Issues after 1965

The planning system set up in 1947 worked. That is to say, it worked in the limited sense of producing a situation which in all its facets and from almost every standpoint was better than the situation before the war. As a technical exercise in ensuring the more efficient functioning of communities, it was an improvement. Another claim is perhaps just as important and easier to substantiate: the overall use of land in England and Wales was more efficient. The most clearly demonstrable aspect of this was the total rate of urbanisation. The rate of over 60,000 acres a year which the Scott Commission had reported dropped, in the post-war years, to under 30,000![1] It seems fair to speculate that if only pre-war controls had operated after the war the rate would have been higher in the comparative economic and demographic boom of the 1950s than it had been in the 1930s. We could infer from this that in the quarter-century after 1947 more than a thousand square miles, or an average sized English county, was 'saved' from urbanisation by the new planning machinery.

Less quantifiable, but more important, were the real achievements of the system; that a reasonable degree of functional efficiency had been combined with the preservation of the character of a large number of both urban and rural areas of great charm and beauty. Academic students of the system, such as Cullingworth and Mandelker, wrote of the system in tones of general approbation. The Planning Advisory Group, setting out to reform planning in 1965, started off from the premise that British planning was a success. They wrote: 'Any review must start with an assessment of the present system, set up under the Town and Country Planning Act of 1947. When introduced, it was the most advanced system in the world and it still retains much of its strength. Its outstanding characteristics are perhaps its comprehensive nature and its cohesion.'[2]

In other words, though there were criticisms of the way the system worked, they were usually that it did not go far enough, or that it was becoming outdated, or that it was insufficiently creative. The criticisms did not imply that the pre-war situation would be preferable. Only occasionally—and scarcely ever from anyone of eminence—were criticisms levelled at the system which allowed the possibility that the situation might be better without the 1947 Act. These were usually of the form that the system worked in an overly conservative way, so as to stultify both architectural and social experiment and progress.[3] In this sense, planners could be criticised for the ways in which they operated the concept of 'amenity' in practice. But this was an unorthodox view. Most people who had an opinion on the subject distrusted architectural (and agricultural) experiment and put their faith in the preservationist aspects of the system.

So far when I have used the word 'planning', I have used it loosely. The successes of the post-1947 system were not really 'planning' successes in the sense in which Geddes and, indeed, many recent planners would use the expression. They would require that planning should be a progressive and over-arching creative form of administration which involved deliberate inter-relations between the physical environment and social and economic systems. In that sense, 1947 established mere development control, not real planning. It was the system of application, response, inquiry and decision which really worked.

If the development plans under the 1947 system were an inadequate basis for planning in that sense, the relationship between plan-formation and effective decision-making was even further removed from over-arching planning. In the first place, the maps in the development plans furnished too precise a set of criteria to be really operated. Planners could not, in all conscience, recommend the rejection of a viable and harmless scheme and the acceptance of a dubious and ugly proposal simply because the latter conformed more closely to the lines on the map. So the relationship between plan and decision became far more flexible. In official words: 'The Plan itself does not directly control the development or acquisition of land, but it sets out policies guiding future land use.'[4] Elsewhere, plans have been described as a 'broad general strategy'. Such 'flexibility' has been looked upon (by Mandelker, for instance) as a distinct advantage of the system, but though the criteria operated in control-decisions in lieu of creative or precise planning may be sensible or generally acceptable, they do not amount to 'planning' in the Geddes sense.

The most widespread objection of all to the planning control relationship was the time taken by planning. The case of Coventry, often regarded as one of the most efficient and progressive planning authorities in the country, was that a plan was prepared by 1951 and submitted to the minister. It was not finally approved until 1957 and had to be revised in 1962. It was not until 1961 that all the 145 authorities in England and Wales possessed fully approved plans. By 1968 there were still two of the fifty-seven Scottish Authorities which had not produced the plans which were required from them under the parallel legislation of 1947. This meant that, as plans were intended to offer strategies for only a twenty-year period, in the first place, there could only be a limited time in which a planning authority had a fully completed and approved plan which it could use. This would have been true even in an era of comparative stability. But this was not such an era; it was a time of enormous expansion in private motor transport with important consequences for the physical shape of areas, for housing and for retail and recreational activities. The overall number of vehicles registered increased in this period from 4·96 million to 10·56 million, an increase of 113 per cent. More significantly for broad planning problems, as opposed to purely transport problems, the number of private cars on the road increased from 2·5 million to 6·55 million, an increase of 161 per cent.[5] This was an expansion on a far vaster scale than before: in the whole of the period 1939-52 the number of cars had risen by only 2 per cent. Nor did the increase show much sign of stopping: indeed by 1972 the number of vehicles had risen to 16·18 million and the number of cars to 12·72 million, the latter being a 93 per cent increase. Between 1952 and 1962 the total road mileage expanded from 185,523 to 196,135 an increase of exactly 5 per cent.[6] Nevertheless, this meant that there were more than two miles of road for every square mile of Britain by 1962 and 53·8 motor vehicles for every mile of road. By 1972 there were to be 76·4 vehicles per mile.

Planning was difficult in two senses. In the first place, neither the planners nor the development plan system were capable of dealing with the overall effects of traffic, as the Buchanan Report, *Traffic in Towns*, pointed out in 1964. But even if they had the capability, the sheer pace of change, combined with the clumsiness of the planning process, would have made the job impossible.

A great deal of time in the process was consumed by the consideration of objections, because the minister was obliged to consider all objections to a plan. There were over 20,000 objections at the inquiry stage of the Greater London Development Plan which had begun with the re-organisation of local government in London in 1963. Some way of limiting or quickening the consideration of objections had to be created. It was almost as if the creators of the system had made a formal mistake about the role of time in the planning process. They had

E

assumed that time was one variable in the definition of efficient planning, that

$$P = f(x,y,z,\mathrm{I}/t \ldots),$$

where P = quality of planning

x, y, z, are variables governing the quality of planning (say the extent of public participation, the functional integration of development, the aesthetic quality of preservation, etc.)

t is time

The real relationship should be

$$P = f(x(\mathrm{I}/t), y(\mathrm{I}/t), z(\mathrm{I}/t) \ldots).$$

The same argument also applied to the use of cost-benefit analysis. 'Good' cost-benefit analysis could be inferior to 'bad' in its effect, simply because it took far longer.

The problem was by no means a technical one, however; it has important political aspects. What the PAG proposed was a speeding up of the planning process by a distinction between 'Structure Plans' which could be ordered, and must be approved, by central government, and local plans (including general 'county plans' as well as more particular projects called 'district plans' and 'action area' plans) which would not have to go through the same process. This distinction was incorporated into the 1968 Town and Country Planning Act. A later document outlined seven functions for the structure plan:

'1. Interpreting national and regional policies.
2. Establishing aims, policies and general proposals.
3. Providing framework for local plans.
4. Indicating action areas.
5. Providing guidance for development control.
6. Providing basis for co-ordinating decisions (though primarily in lieu of action areas).
7. Bringing main planning issues before minister and public.'[7]

Interpretations of the political content of this reform have been varied. Thomas Sharp said in 1966: 'the PAG report is a hopelessly unbalanced and dangerous document'.[8] He argued that the report was written solely so as to make planning easier for the planners. He was suspicious of the membership of the group: nineteen local and central government officials, two consultants, yet only six practising professional planners. Sharp was especially suspicious of the possibility that local plans would often not be prepared at all and the structure plan would be used as a basis for action. He expressed himself in strong terms:

'I must say that I am astonished that an allegedly responsible body of men—90 per cent of them public servants at that—should in this day and age make such recommendations towards authoritarianism. Where are we living? In Russia? In China? That it is all directed against the rights and interests of the individual is perfectly clear.'[9]

Objections which sound fairly similar were registered by the Chairman of the CPRE in a letter to *The Times* about the Town and Country Planning Bill 1968. To him it was a Bill which 'sets the stage for silencing effective comment on environmental change . . . a wholly retrograde step and a challenge to civil liberties'.[10] But the criticisms diverge sharply, because the CPRE statement emphasises the increased independence of local authorities in the reformed system. Local authorities cannot be a fair judge because of their 'own pecuniary involvement in development proposals'. In some respects it could be inferred that the system was reviving aspects of the situation between 1933 and 1939. There are shades in this argument of John Stuart Mill's preference of an enlightened, national élite over an ignorant and self-interested local élite.[11]

It is perhaps odd that this Bill and the fears it aroused of authoritarianism should be discussed at precisely the same time as demands for greater 'participation' in planning were being mooted. It was in this year that the Skeffington Committee on participation met and reported. There were some objections to 'paternalist' planning from the planners themselves. E. C. Hargrove reported in his study of professional innovators in English politics that the two main objections that the younger, brighter planners had to the existing system were its emphasis on maps and architecture on the one hand, and its élitist authoritarianism on the other. According to one (unnamed) planner, the system could be typified as a double act of 'Sir Patrick Abercrombie and the old LCC'.[12]

The government in general, and perhaps the ministry in particular, could be accused of inconsistency or even dishonesty. They were claiming to both increase and decrease participation. Such trickery and confusion are possible in governments, of course. But in this case the accusation would be unfair. The two arguments can be made consistent without resorting to pedantry.

The HMSO manual states that: 'The structure plan will be the means of bringing the authority's intentions, and the reasoning behind those intentions to the attention of the Minister and the public.'[13] Elsewhere, it is insisted that: 'The statement of the new-style structure plan will differ, therefore, from its predecessor in that *summarised* substantiation of the decisions will be required, including description of the examination of alternative decisions that may have been considered.'[14] The document can be accused of authoritarianism in that the plan and the planners should state aims and leave only the consideration of strategies still open:

'Although aims should be sufficiently precise to guide the plan in a specific direction, they should offer room for the examination of alternative strategies that might, to a greater or lower extent, achieve them. A statement of aims will be valuable as a broad indication of what the plan is trying to do and the direction which should be taken by the changes it proposes; it will serve to secure the co-ordination of the policies and proposals in the plan. Without this statement the authority, the public and the Minister will have difficulty in judging the value of individual decisions that make up the strategy.'[15]

In one sense this rubric has allowed of a greater degree of participation than ever before. Most local authorities have, since 1968 at least, made sincere attempts at encouraging participation, particularly in the form of surveys which ask people, for instance, which of three broad strategies for expansion their town should adopt. Public meetings have been used to debate similar issues. Neither response nor effect have been impressive, but it is still arguable that the public has more real opportunities to express opinions than before. What went on before 1968 was largely the mere expression of what Barry calls privately oriented wants, or interests. The 20,000 objections to the Greater London development plan contain a vast majority from individuals and groups whose property or immediate personal environment is affected. The great majority of the remainder are from established pressure groups. Only a limited few are from individuals without vested interests. Although privately oriented wants are perfectly valid consideration for decision-making in general, there are some strong arguments against considering them too fully in planning:

1. *The expressed interests are self-cancelling if they concern the siting of a project.* Nobody wants an urban through-way near them. A will argue that it should run past B's house; B will argue it should run past A's. Twenty thousand objections may tell as nothing about public opinion except that the public consists of selfish individuals.

2. *Expressed interests may be unrepresentative.* If participation is concerned with broader issues—say whether a project should exist at all—it seems reasonable (both on prioristic and empirical grounds) that only those most affected by its benefits and disbenefits will actually act. A project which is clearly good to the planner might meet with only objections, because its benefits, though real, are too thinly spread to attract much support. This has occurred, for instance, where the closing of a shopping street to private vehicles has met with only objections from inhabitants of residential streets through which traffic was directed, even though it was a generally popular move. People who are only slightly affected rarely act. There is a case, contrary to Sharp, for protecting the public from the rights of individuals.

3. *The expression of private interests is uninformative.* In many important ways, we all *know* what people want from their environment. They want privacy, community, a good view, a short journey to work, an appreciating property, convenient retail outlets, adequate recreational facilities, and a beautiful landscape. That they react in defence of any of these tells us nothing. Roy Gregory has pointed out the absurdity of the public meeting held by the Ministry Inspector before the Inquiry into the Holme Pierrepoint Power Station.[16] He wanted to assess the local opinion. But any reasonable man knows that no other reasonable man wants a power station near his dwelling. Yet if we want electricity, someone must suffer. Complex problems—both of maximisation and distribution—are involved, and the lodging of individual objections will never help solve them.

So public discussion of strategy should help to elicit genuine information about public preferences. To do so it must remain at the level of arguing about whether there should be a road running north-west from the centre of the town, without a map saying exactly where the road should go. Or it should offer choices as to whether development should take place north of the town and preservation south or vice versa, without allowing it to be clear whose property will be affected. This will not always be possible, and there will still be fundamental criticism of the system, but it has a distinct theoretical superiority over the unreformed system.

THE DEPARTMENT OF THE ENVIRONMENT AND THE REFORM OF LOCAL GOVERNMENT

At this point it is necessary to mention two other important changes; the establishment of the Department of the Environment in 1970 and the re-organisation of local government, effective from 1974. I use the word 'mention' deliberately because that is all I intend to do in this context. The exact import of these reforms on environmental planning is difficult to estimate at this stage.

The Department of Environment has been rationalised in terms which would have been familiar to those involved in the planning conferences of the Second World War; indeed, it is, in effect, close to Abercrombie's idea of a 'suzerain ministry' for planning. It is intended to eliminate many kinds of conflicting and ill co-ordinated policies from central government's environmental planning. To this end it combines three ministries (Housing and Construction, Local Government and Development and Transport Industries) which are headed by junior ministers under the Department headed by a Secretary of State of Cabinet rank. However slowly or partially the administrative integration of functions may have proceeded,[17] the constitutional change was an important one. A far wider range of government policies affecting the environment was brought under the same chain of responsibility. Thus a single minister became responsible for, and had to defend in Cabinet and Parliament, not only the working of the basic planning structure, but also policies for roads, air traffic and public transport.

The Redcliffe-Maud Commission on Local Government in England,[18] which reported in June 1969, also specifically claimed to offer rational-isations of government structures which would aid planning efficiency. Its general aims were to enhance both the efficiency of local government service provision and the democratic quality of local politics by creating local areas which were more viable, that is to say far more compatible with modern patterns of mobility, than were the 1888 areas. To this end it proposed unitary authorities, including both large towns and their surrounding areas, except in the case of Merseyside, SELNEC (that is to say, SE Lancs and NE Cheshire—in effect, Greater Manchester), and Greater Birmingham, which should be two-tier 'metropolitan' areas. These were to allow greater integration of control and economies of large scale in service provision and to be more attractive politically, both to the voter and to the potential councillor.

There were some conservationist fears that this change, particularly in handing control of the hinterlands to the major conurbations, would simply allow urbanisation which would be greater in total and less well planned than before. Not everybody believed this; Stanley Jeeves, full-time Secretary of the Lancashire Branch of the CPRE, argued that cities might well achieve more than the old counties with their rural surroundings, especially in projects for recreational land and the clearance of derelict areas.[19] However, the issue was never resolved, because the eventual system of the 1972 Local Government Act minimised the land controlled by metropolitan areas, although it did establish three new ones in West Yorkshire, South Yorkshire and Tyneside.

The general arguments of the Redcliffe-Maud Commission were to apply specifically to planning. Under the heading, 'Better Services', and the sub-heading, 'Planning and Transportation', they argued that:

'As the number of people and cars constantly increases, questions of land use—for housing and schools, industry, commerce and transporta-tion—will continue to become more complicated; but in the new and larger local government areas it will be possible (as it is not today) to work out and apply coherent plans for meeting the challenge of present and future local problems.

Among the chief of these are finding room for the new houses, clearing slums, renewing urban centres, fostering new employment opportunities, deciding what additional roads are needed, determining the balance between private and public transport, and trying to reconcile development with the use of the countryside for agriculture and recreation.'[20]

The means of achieving these aims is considerably modified in the Conservative legislation of 1972. The main difference is that planning functions are divided between two tiers, the county and district. Put simply, the counties (including the six metropolitan areas) are to be responsible for structure plans, and the districts for local plans and responses to planning applications. This relationship is an ambiguous one; it is difficult to predict how it will work in practice. For given the different sorts of local plan, the different rates of submission of local plans and, indeed, the possibility that they may not be necessary for some areas, which is allowed for under the 1968 Act, the relationship may work differently in different areas. Such an outcome may well be a good thing. In areas where the county is a viable administrative entity and has a good planning department, and the towns are relatively small, the county may well be the dominant planning authority. Lancashire may well present this type of relationship. In other areas where districts were previously large county boroughs with good planning departments, those districts may well continue as effective planning authorities. This might be the role of Coventry inside the West Midlands Metropolitan County.

IDEOLOGICAL ISSUES IN PLANNING

Throughout the period from the late 1950s issues were developing in planning which were not, and could not be, covered by structural reform. These concerned the criteria, rather than the process, of planning. As the pressures on the environment from changing social patterns, from economic growth and technological progress intensified, so did the dilemmas which planners faced between gains in measurable economic efficiency and corresponding hygienic, social and aesthetic losses. The 1971 HMSO manual on structure planning sees these dilemmas as crucial to planning:

'Efficiency and environment run like threads, often crossing each other, right through the process as the plan is refined from broad intentions, through aims, to the strategy and detailed changes, and it is really a matter of judgement how best to give scope for the creation of both. Thus the aims for efficiency and environment may be in conflict, even mutually exclusive; for example, easy access by motor car to the town centre may be incompatible with the conservation of its architectural quality.'[21]

These problems were emphasised and brought to public attention by a series of lengthy and dramatic cases throughout the period. Five of these cases are described by Roy Gregory in *The Price of Amenity*. Although the issues in each case, as they were agreed in practice, were extremely complicated, Gregory concluded that there was a common theme, a basic irresoluble, common to all of them. It was this: how were non-marketable environmental benefits such as beauty and tranquillity (loosely and generally referred to as 'amenity') to be evaluated against economic efficiency. A further, though related question, brought out clearly by the case of the Abingdon Gas Holder,[22] was distributive: given agreement that a quantifiable economic cost should be met in securing a degree of preservation, how should the cost be borne? Gas consumers, ratepayers and taxpayers were all candidates in the Abingdon case.

This kind of planning problem gradually came to be seen to raise issues of a different order from functional planning or planning within a broad consensus. These issues were most widely outlined in the long saga of the Third London Airport. The 'judgement' called for in the manual is not of a sort for which planners are trained nor of a sort in which they have any special rights or expertise. It involves aesthetic evaluations and ideological positions. The 1968 Town and Country Planning Act did offer a partial solution in that the minister could set up 'Planning Inquiry Commissions' into important and controversial cases. That provision did not itself offer any acceptable criteria or theory of planning; it only offered a broader structure within which such criteria could be more adequately considered. In any case the provision is, as yet, a dead letter.

At this stage of the debate the academic study of politics has most to offer for an understanding of planning. The political theorist's task is to explain and analyse as clearly as possible the ideological dimensions and dilemmas of environmental issues.

NOTES

1. See R. H. Best and J. T. Coppock, *The Changing Use of Land in Britain* (London, Faber, 1962).
2. Planning Advisory Group, *The Future of Development Plans* (London, HMSO, 1965), 1:6–1:7.
3. One such view is discussed in Chapter 7 under the heading, 'The Market Re-Visited : Non-Plan'.
4. Central Office of Information, *Town and Country Planning in Britain*, Reference Pamphlet 9 (London, HMSO, 1972), p. 5.
5. British Road Federation, *Basic Road Statistics 1973*, Table 1, pp. 2–3; percentile calculations by the author.
6. Ibid., Table 5, p. 18.

7. *Development Plans: A Manual on Form and Content* (London, HMSO 1971), 3:10.
8. Thomas Sharp, 'Planning Planning', in *Journal of the Town Planning Institute*, Vol. 52 (1966), p. 209.
9. Ibid., p. 210.
10. *The Times* (30 January 1968).
11. J. S. Mill, 'Centralisation', in *Edinburgh Review* (1862), pp. 323-88.
12. E. C. Hargrove, 'Tradition and Change in England', in *Comparative Politics*, Vol. 4, No. 4 (1972).
13. *Development Plans: A Manual on Form and Content*, 7:4.
14. Ibid., 3:12.
15. Ibid., 4:11.
16. R. Gregory, *The Price of Amenity* (London, Macmillan, 1971), pp. 89-132.
17. See, for instance, articles by John Clare in *The Times* (8, 9 and 10 May 1972).
18. *Report of the Royal Commission on Local Government in England* (Chairman, Lord Redcliffe-Maud), Cmnd 4040 (London, HMSO, 1969).
19. To the author privately in an interview in June 1969.
20. *Short Version of the Report of the Royal Commission on Local Government in England*, Cmnd. 4039 (London, HMSO, 1969), p. 14.
21. *Development Plans: A Manual on Form and Content*, 4:17.
22. Gregory, op. cit., pp. 245-95.

Chapter 7

Political Theory and Planning: The Orthodoxy

MODERNISED BENTHAMISM

The principles which for the most part dominate modern planning. or, for that matter, administration, in Britain are to be found in a single book: Jeremy Bentham's *Principles of Morals and Legislation*.[1] To many minds this claim might seem an overly trite example of Lord Keynes's accusation that most men who described themselves as 'practical' and therefore uninterested in theory were themselves 'the slaves of some defunct economist'. For we live in a very complex society, one which produces (and permits) a multitude of ideologies and theories, which allows a hundred answers to every possible question. It seems perverse to argue that a single doctrine, apparently outdated, which in any case had little or no influence on planning in the century following its most famous exposition, can furnish an approach to modern problems which successfully prevails over others.

Nevertheless, I would argue that liberal, empirical Benthamism does furnish such a prevailing theoretical approach. I prefer the appellation, 'Benthamism' to that of 'Utilitarianism' because in restoring the major premises and arguments of Bentham to intellectual respectability, one of the main casualties has been the concept of utility itself. Both this development and my general argument can best be illustrated by outlining the structure of modern Benthamism. This can be done in terms of six principles.

1. *Real individual preferences are the only proper ends.* At the outset, this is an assertion of teleology against deontology. Ultimate justifications are to be in terms of an end achieved or a purpose, not in terms of duties or of deeds good-in-themselves. This applies especially to public policies. Bentham wrote that: 'Nature has placed mankind under the

governance of two sovereign masters—pleasure and pain. It is for them alone to point out what we ought to do as well as to determine what we shall do.'[2] Locke, Hume and, arguably, Hobbes were earlier, if less overt, examples of this tradition of private and public morality; it developed, too, in eighteenth- and nineteenth-century economic theory, particularly English and Scottish economic theory. One of Bentham's immediate targets in attacking deontology was the political philosophy of lawyers, primarily Blackstone. But it is more interesting to see Bentham as the critic of a much wider tradition including Kantianism and a great deal of Christian theology. There is some evidence that Bentham's writings had considerable influence on radical and anti-clerical movements, mainly in the Spanish-speaking world.

However, there is more in common between Bentham's statement and the modern principle than their being teleological rather than deontological. Empiricism is common to both in that the criteria of morality are to reduce to something which can actually be demonstrated; an end product to which we can point. Deontology is to be criticised in both cases for its methodological as well as its moral failings. The content of duties is insufficiently 'hard'. More importantly, both approaches stress the importance of the real individual. Genuine ends can be conceived only as the satisfaction of wants by existing individual human beings. Bentham was explicit, in the 'deontology' that dead people, ideal people, mythical people, even unborn people, were of no account in morality. This is emphasised, too, in the modern version, though few would agree with Bentham about the unborn.

2. *Real individual preferences are derived from hypothetical choices.*
Bentham offered a set of variables for determining the level of pleasure in an individual, including 'propinquity', 'fecundity' and duration. Economists such as Marshall treated utility as if it were quantifiable; the measurement was 'utils' and the law of diminishing marginal utility was a necessary relationship between an individual and a good or benefit. It states that as an individual receives units of a good or benefit one after another, there must come a point at which the utility of the last unit is less than the utility of the one which preceded it.

But no progress was made on measuring utility in practice. As with many other important concepts in social science we can use it loosely in clear-cut cases (for instance, to say that x would get more pleasure or utility from receiving a bicycle than he would from receiving a book token for his birthday). However, in all the important cases—where we have a dilemma to resolve—such intuition is inadequate. Yet there are no criteria for statements about pleasure and pain except the biological tests and these would be absurd grounds for policy. At one level the criticism amounts to saying that Utilitarianism is not much help to us in the formation of policy, but in philosophical hands such as those of A. J. Ayer, the criticism could be deeper.[3] It could involve questioning the logical status of any statements about utility, of relegating utility to the 'meaningless' category.

In order, therefore, to have a coherent and philosophically respectable Benthamism it was necessary to replace the concept of utility by something else; this is perhaps the intellectual equivalent of the process of 'repointing' brickwork, in that the rotten parts are taken out and replaced without the identity of the structure being changed. In effect, utility was replaced by the hypothetical choice model. The ultimate justification for one action rather than another is that individuals would, on the whole, prefer it. The criterion offers a test, at least in principle. When we talk of preference, we are talking of the alternative situation an individual would choose, if choice were open to him.

3. *Real individual preferences are related transitively.* Hypothesising individual choices only tells us that a given person has an indefinite number of relationships between sets of two alternatives, one of which he prefers or between which he is indifferent. By assuming that these preferences are related transitively, we can proceed on to a more practical footing and construct a preference order for any individual. The assumption itself is this: for any three alternatives, A, B, C, and any person, x, if x prefers A to B and B to C, then x prefers A to C. It is difficult to specify a reason for the assumption. 1 is a value-judgement—indeed it is what Bergson, in welfare economics, classed as 'the fundamental value judgement'.[4] 2 is a methodological interpretation of 1, arguably the only logically proper interpretation. But what grounds are there for assuming transitivity? One new problem is that it seems, in the real world, to be false in a way that the first two assumptions could not be. People are, in practice, confused in such a way as to have intransitively related preferences. There are still, however, strong arguments for assuming transitivity. Let us take the simplest case of preferences which are related in a non-transitive, or circular, fashion—the boy who prefers an ice cream to an ice lolly, an ice lolly to a bar of chocolate, and a bar of chocolate to an ice cream. Whatever he is given, there is something he would have preferred. But his satisfaction (or dissatisfaction) cannot be expressed coherently. No system of allocation could claim to be the 'right' thing for the boy, so it is a trivial criticism of a system involving the assumption of transitivity that it cannot. We must assume the transitivity of preferences.

4. *Real individual preferences are connexed.* So far the model has assumed that the preferences of real individuals are uniquely worthy of satisfaction, that these preferences must be derived from real choices or

the best hypothesis about choices, and that preferences are related transitively. Thus the wants that men have can be said to fall into preference structures, tables of ordered comparison.

But on the basis of the assumptions so far there is no limit to the number of preference-tables an individual can have, which is the same as saying that not all preferences are related the one to the other. Without some new assumption we still have no possible grounds for making a decision in many of the real dilemmas which confront us. Supposing a man has a set of preferences relevant to his productive role and also a set for his private life. The former might involve him preferring the peace and quiet of the storeroom to working on the track to such an extent that he will accept ten pounds less a week for doing so. At home he might prefer living in a 'better' area to the possession of a motor car. It is necessary, though, to insist that all possible benefits and disbenefits should be related. Particularly in 'environmental' issues we must constantly compare 'environmental' benefits (which might include beauty, community, familiarity and tranquillity) with 'material' benefits (personal wealth, facility of travel, safety, etc.). These are comparisons which individual human beings may not often have to make.

The assumption of connexity is this: that any two possible benefits to an individual can be conceived as hypothetical alternatives and related as preferences. Many possible benefits have a monetary value, so money is a relation to any preference—one which is indefinitely divisible and allows a bundle of marketable goods of one's own choice. Because any benefit can be compared to any other by an individual, so any benefit can be related to money. We have reached the point where our assumptions allow us to ask a man: 'How much money would you prefer to the continued existence of your wife?'

Thus the assumption of connexity has dramatic implications. It is the same as saying: 'Nothing is sacred. There are no totems. Everything in life must be subjected to the real preference test.'

Many of the criticisms made of the assumption are rather trivial. It is a 'childish' way of looking at things in so far as resembles some of the things children say and do. Small boys do ask each other, 'Would you let your sister die if it meant you could play for England?', and they have been known to ask God if He will make their mummy better if they give up eating sweets. It is also a callous way of looking at things in so far as it insists on the implication that the 'spiritual', 'personal' facets of life are at least comparable with the material and the mundane.

The defence must be that the callousness is part of life, not of the model. Harsh decisions must be made, both by individuals and by governments. Individuals do find it necessary to accept danger, separation from their families, even ill-health in return for money. As a public we choose to allow death and danger (by miners, say, or drivers) in order that we might have more material benefits. Comparisons must be made in order that decisions can be made in a non-arbitrary manner. In a secular society nothing is acceptably sacred, nothing is immune from such comparison.

The assumption of connexity is, of course, morally equivalent to Bentham's assertion that: 'The quantity of pleasure being equal, pushpin is as good as poetry.' In the modern equivalent, it reads: 'The quantity of monetary-equivalent being equal, potash is as good as beauty.'

5. *The aggregate level of preference—attainment can be derived from inter-personal comparison and addition.* Steps 1-4, taken together, give us coherent answers to questions about what should be done for any individual; they constitute a Liberal-Utilitarian account of individual interests. They do not, in themselves, tell us how to aggregate individual interests, how to make governmental decisions. The typical problem, for a two-person situation, is this: there are two individuals, A and B. There are two possible alternatives, x and y. x and y constitute either the only possible alternatives or they constitute alternatives either of which both A and B would prefer to any alternative except the other. x satisfies A's preferences more than y. y satisfies B's preferences more than x. x and y are not compatible. What is to be done?

We need some form of quantitative comparison such that we can say that the difference between x and y is greater for A than it is for B, therefore x would leave them, collectively, better off than y. It is not easy to find one, except in intuitively easy cases where we could make a decision without a formal argument. This is the problem of inter-personal comparison and it has long been the major intellectual stumbling-block of Utilitarianism. Indeed, some writers have 'refused' before this fence. These include Vilfredo Pareto, who argued that the only acceptable definition of a social optimum was a situation in which no individual can be made better off without some other individual being made worse off. Even where we can make a hundred individuals better off whilst only making one worse off, we cannot categorically justify such a policy. Some examples of doing this—torturing a man for the amusement of an audience, for instance—demand our rejection.

The 'Pareto-optimum' tells us only what we must not do; it can allow an indefinite number of plausible alternatives which can be considered as optimising policies. For instance, almost all taxation policies could be considered as Pareto-optimal. However, a logical technique has been developed for reducing this situation to a single optimum solution. This is the 'compensation principle' developed by J. R. Hicks and N. Kaldor.[5] If we can show that if x rather than y is implemented those who gain from x rather than y can compensate those who lose, we can work out a single optimum. Compensation means the 'losers' being given something such that they prefer x-plus-compensation to y. Accurate compensation becomes possible because of connexity; we can normally hypothesise a monetary sum so that any individual can be 'offered' a bundle of marketable goods.

Two examples. Firstly, in the torture case, if we can acquaint the performer with the exact nature and consequence of his performance and offer him a fee which he is prepared to accept drawn from the prices the audience have paid for the performance, then the show can be justified. Secondly, let us suppose a planning inquiry commission is faced with the problem of whether to build an airport outside a city. This is to be a 'yes or no' question, not the Roskill Commission's problem of siting an airport. People will gain from the airport in terms of easier and safer travelling for business and holidays. These gains can be given monetary values; in so far as they stimulate the economy, locally and nationally, almost everybody might gain. But some people will also lose—by their houses being destroyed, by the noise of aeroplanes, by losing an area which they considered beautiful, by their community being fragmented. If we can discover who is losing what and how much it would need for them to consider that having the airport would be preferable given the other things we are giving them, and if the airport can generate sufficient wealth to do this, then it is better to build it. It does not matter, of course, that compensation should be paid, only that it could be paid, to show that the airport is aggregatively beneficial. The practical objections to 'compensation' (that we can never satisfactorily discover the appropriate level) are not objections to the principle. By using compensation as a hypothesis, we can therefore claim to make aggregative decisions.

6. *Correct decisions maximise aggregate preference—attainment.* Bentham wrote: 'The only proper end and purpose of government is to achieve the greatest happiness of the greatest number.' It is the purpose of this last step to prescribe that optimal policies, as defined by 1-5, should be implemented in practice and not over-ridden by external consideratons nor allowed to remain impractical.

THE MODEL AND THE REAL WORLD

I have argued that liberal Benthamism prevails in our culture and I have presented liberal Benthamism as a complex structure of premise and inference which requires, in order to be rescued from damaging criticism, some sophisticated logical moves. There is an apparent contradiction in these two arguments because few people understand the structure as I have presented it. In the actual form I have presented it, it is original.

The contradiction is superficial. We do not expect everybody to be acquainted with the paradigm of physical explanation in their culture, the mode of physics. Very few are. Yet it remains the paradigm of physics and we must refer to it if we are to fully understand why a doctor or a motor mechanic acts as he does. In the same way the majority of citizens of the Soviet Union do not understand more than a small part of the theoretical ramifications of Marxism-Leninism. Even so, it will help us to understand them if we understand more of their prevailing ideology than they do themselves. Liberal Benthamism in the real world involves political and administrative responses of varying complexity, but we must understand its workings with reference to the full version.

When I say 'culture', I mean three things, all of them in principle observable. First of all I mean general attitudes and approaches to private matters by individuals making statements about what they or others ought to do. I am not saying that all moral comments are Benthamite, but I am saying that the more completely thought out and argued they are the more likely they are to be Benthamite. See, for example, the 'agony' columns of women's magazines where solutions to dilemmas are always overtly Benthamite: the recommended course of action is rationalised as being that which will make those involved happiest in the end. Secondly, there is the familiar concept of the political culture—in Beer's phrase: '. . . the images and sentiments which function as operative ideas within a community'.[6] And lastly, more relevantly, there is the 'administrative culture', the basic beliefs of those making administrative decisions about the general purpose and status of administration and about the techniques and criteria of decision-making. It is in the administrative culture that liberal Benthamism as a doctrine prevails most clearly.

One account of the importance of Benthamite doctrines of political economy in understanding politics is in Professor W. J. M. Mackenzie's *Politics and Social Science*.[7] He argues that: 'Political Economy has from the first been concerned with the maximisation of some collective entity or other.'[8] There is a gap between theory in practice, he asserts, in that 'Bentham's "felicific calculus" is as dead as the general social welfare function. But we go on arguing in real life as if they were still alive. . . .'[9] I disagree with the first statement and agree with the second. The disagreement is a question of identity. For I regard the arguments I have explicated as being a new version of the 'felicific calculus', not an alternative to it.

Mackenzie outlines three main sets of beliefs as to how maximisation of the collective entity is to be achieved: 'A' is 'faith in the market'. The classical economists' belief that the market mechanism, by allowing individuals free play to pursue their interests, acts as a mechanism for ensuring the maximisation of the sum of all interests. This was abandoned following the development of oligopoly and trade cycle theories.

'B' is 'the general social welfare function'. The dissatisfaction with the market mechanism led to a call for maximising decisions from above and the development in academic economics of various forms of general welfare function in an attempt to set out criteria governing all 'correct' decision-making. Heavily attacked, and almost defeated, as welfare economics this approach has had a considerable revival as cost-benefit analysis.

'C' is 'the logic of economic politics'. Since the war there has been, in effect, a revival of Utilitarian democratic theory, in the belief (expressed here in a highly general form) that ways of giving people what they want can only be defined in terms of political procedures and not in terms of the administrative criteria of decision-making. One of the most formal and explicit works in this revival is to be found in Anthony Downs's *An Economic Theory of Democracy*.[10]

To be clear, I should point out that Mackenzie puts greater emphasis on another three-fold distinction, that between the general social welfare function, the logic of economic politics and the transitional stage between the two. He only mentions in passing the distinction I have emphasised. However, my purpose in outlining the above distinction is to put into perspective some of the arguments and proposals which have been put forward in relation to environmental planning in the last few years.

META-PLANNING: ALTERNATIVE CRITERIA FOR PLANNING

1. *The market revisited: 'Non-Plan'*. In 1969 Peter Hall and others published a set of articles in *New Society* under the general title of 'Non-Plan: An Experiment in Freedom'.[11] The tone of the articles can be judged by their introductory statements. 'Town and country planning', they say, 'has today become an unquestioned shibboleth. Yet few of its procedures or value-judgements have any sound basis except delay. Why not have the courage, where practical, to let people shape their own environment?'

Letting people shape their own environment is defined as the dismantling of the planning system. Among the consequences of such freedom which the authors envisage are:

'Strip cities' along the edges of main roads;
'fun parks' in places like the New Forest. These would include tree-top level cable car rides and artificial lakes stocked for fishermen paying high fees;

F

garages which are also large, neon-lit, entertainment areas providing a variety of amusement.

The authors use many of the familiar arguments of *laissez-faire.* Imposing 'good taste' through planning is merely a restrictive snobbery, they claim, for many of the most admired features of our environment have come into being as the accidental consequence of some obscure private whim. The commitment to pushpin rather than poetry is overt; the quantity of pleasure being equal, fun palaces are as good as forests. Professor Hall, certainly, operates an almost biological concept of pleasure. Elsewhere, he compares the frustration and misery on the faces of those obliged to spend their day out picnicking on the verge of the road with the measurable satisfaction which would be found in a properly organised, privately run, country park.[12]

Conservation, under 'Non-Plan', would stand or fall according to the strength of demand for it. If people really want to maintain areas of solitude and wilderness, speculators will buy up large tracts of land and preserve them, charging entrance fees for admission.

It is difficult to tell how seriously the authors take themselves. Much of this collection of articles is written in a fairly light-hearted vein and, in any case, they only envisage 'Non-Plan' as being applied to a number of limited, though large, areas. So it would perhaps be too pompous to bring the whole weight of mixed-economy objections to bear. But one objection to the market-mechanism is clear, and special to the case. It is that leisure-demands are changing measurably and over the short period with changes in education and opportunities. Environmental changes are often irreversible: a landscape once destroyed cannot be re-created. The chances of producing a counter-productive result by exposure to market forces would therefore seem to be enormous.

2. The general social welfare function re-visited: cost-benefit analysis. A great deal of discussion about planning and administration in the last few years has been devoted to cost-benefit analysis. This is hardly surprising; if my analysis of prevailing norms and doctrines of decision-making is correct, cost-benefit analysis constitutes almost a logical limiting case of orthodox moral assumptions. However, it should be made clear that not all cost-benefit analysis is the same: there is clearly an important difference between the analysis as a technique of decision-making and as an aid to decision-making.

Cost-benefit as an over-riding technique has been most severely criticised, particularly as used by the Roskill Commission. In the Commission's defence it should be said (and has often been said) that the Commission was not asked to make an overall decision, but to make a strategic decision within an overall political commitment; viz. that there should be a Third London Airport. However, within that framework assessment was made of all the possible aspects of each site under consideration in terms of 'cost'. In principle the equation operated was:

Minimum cost = maximum utility = correct decision

Evidence was taken based on the compensation principle in order to estimate the importance of aircraft noise as a disadvantage. Loss of land was costly according to agricultural production. The most notorious evaluation was the equation of the Norman parish church in Stukely with its fire insurance value. On to the compensation figures was built a 'distributional value' to even up any bias in individuals' compensation equations which might be the consequence of unequal income; this last can easily be seen as an interpretation of Bentham's stipulation that: 'Each is to count for one and no one is to count for more than one.'

There have been serious and widespread academic objections to the sort of equations implied by the connexity assumption and by this kind of cost-benefit analysis. Professor Hall described the Roskill Commission as 'the apotheosis of Utilitarianism'[13] (though his real objection must be to its paternalism) and Professor Self has accused it of strengthening 'the existing tendency to convert genuine political and social issues into bogus technical ones'.[14]

Since the period of academic criticism of the Roskill exercise, however, cost-benefit analysis has been interpreted in many instances in a more partial way—as only one kind of evidence relevant to the making of decisions. This can be done by attaching a rider to the analysis which admits that some factors (beauty, for instance) were not included in the calculation. This status was attributed to cost-benefit by the Departmental Statement of Case to the public inquiry on the Banbury-Birmingham section of the M40 held at Kenilworth in 1972. Alternatively, the analysis can involve merely deciding on certain values and finding out whether an investment can be justified in terms of these values. For instance, the Department of the Environment has recommended to local authorities that the cost of deaths in road accidents varies from £20,000 to £24,000 to enable them to discover whether a road safety investment is justifiable.[15]

3. *Quasi-judicial: the public interest.* There is a sort of paradox about cost-benefit analysis: it is itself a costly exercise (Roskill, for instance, cost many millions of pounds) which is not worth doing except for important decisions. For less important instances the cost of costing can be too high just as for an individual it may be better to make a quick and easy decision about how to spend his evening than to agonise towards a fully coherent decision.

It is the duty of ministry inspectors at public inquiries to produce recommendations as to the public interest in a planning case. To help him make his recommendations, the inspector carries with him a rather light conceptual tool kit, the main items in which are 'amenity' and 'the public interest'. He must first decide whether the interests of 'amenity' are threatened by a development. If he considers that they are threatened, he must then decide whether the probable economic gains are sufficient to outweigh the loss of amenity. If they are, the development is in 'the public interest'; if not, not. Or at least that is how a model decision would be made, barring the more pragmatic political considerations, some of which are brought to life in Gregory's case studies.

Gregory also concludes that public inquiries (and other decision procedures in the system) are really doing the same thing as cost-benefit analysis. He concludes that: 'The familiar public inquiry and Private Bill procedure does partially reproduce some of the features of cost-benefit analysis.'[16]

4. *The market reformed: Mishanism.* If Hall *et al.* envisage the market situation bringing into being a radically transformed, 'modern' environment for a leisure class equivalent to the whole population, Dr E. J. Mishan, starting from a similar theoretical base, envisages scarcely any change at all. Whereas the Roskill Commission debated the costs of alternative airport sites, Mishan argues that a realistic assessment of total costs would result in the abolition of aeroplanes altogether. He is a hard-line conservationist. Take, for example, this statement from his first book on the subject: 'Sustained technological advance . . . tends inexorably to destroy the sources of satisfaction of ordinary people regardless of the form of economic or social organisation.'[17]

The case is expanded in Mishan's article, 'The Spillover Enemy',[18] and in his later book, *Growth: The Price We Pay.*[19] 'Spillovers are bad effects of economic growth which are not taken into account when either firms or governments make decisions. They include pollution, ecological change, and the loss of available beauty and tranquillity both from industrial spillover and from tourist spillover.' Modern agricultural methods such as the use of pesticides and the elimination of hedges are a good example of spillovers: costs such as the deterioration of the aesthetic appeal of landscape, ecological effects on adjacent land with a different use, and eventual deterioration of the 'improved' land itself (through, for instance, 'dust bowl' effects) are taken into account neither by the farmer in his costing nor by the Ministry of Agriculture when it encourages 'modernisation'.

Mishan considers several possible methods of dealing with the problem of balancing spillovers and economic gains. The solution he prefers in *The Spillover Enemy* centres on the notions of 'amenity right' and 'private space'. Surveys should establish the general levels of compensation appropriate when individuals are affected by noise, pollution or loss of landscape. Civil law should then be changed so that individuals can sue other individuals or firms for loss of amenity consequent upon an invasion of their private space. There would thus be an active discouragement to polluters of the environment and destroyers of the landscape well within the working of the market mechanism. Prices would rise, but we should, in the end, get what we really want.

On the level of theory it is implausible to contest that spillovers exist and that they are underestimated in the costing procedures of both public and private organisations. Translating that analysis into practice (or, for that matter, taking Mishan's own practical remedies seriously) is a different matter. The practical problems are daunting. Imagine setting out the private space framework for a council estate and dealing with the amenity-right cases which follow. The operation only becomes conceivable if we assume the inhabitants to have identical tastes and interests. I rather think that Mishan does make this assumption and that he assumes also that popular tastes and interests are identical with his own.

However, his terminology (and his plan) seemed to find a sympathetic response among politicians, particularly, but not exclusively, in the Conservative party. In an interview in March 1970 Christopher Chataway said: 'A Conservative Government will accept the principle that it is the duty of contemporary society to pay the full price for what it consumes . . . if a factory takes clean water out of a river and puts it back polluted it is failing to meet one integral part of production costs'.[20] Similar sentiments were expressed by Peter Walker at the 1970 Party Conference, while on the Labour side Douglas Jay's article, 'The Cost of Urban Motorways',[21] is heavily laced with Mishanite terminology and conclusions.

Cynically, one might suggest that this terminology is ideal for politicians. It acknowledges the problem, lies well within the liberal culture, yet sidesteps the need for direct action.

5. *Three kinds of politics.* There are a range of theories about how to make planning decisions which come under the broad heading of politics. The two most important of these—the increase of mass participation and the systematic involvement of pressure groups—will be discussed in detail in Chapters 9 and 10. But a third is worth reflecting on; it is what Professor Self offers us as an alternative to cost-benefit analysis under the heading of 'planning'. This involves 'judgements made according to some mixture of goods to be achieved or values maximised' and a 'co-ordinated framework of policy considerations which should guide the choice of alternatives'.[22]

This is sensible, but negative—in the best sense of both those words. It takes us back to our starting-point, perhaps asking the same questions in a more sophisticated way. How are goals to be mixed? How is the co-ordinated framework of policy considerations to be interpreted? We can only answer these questions by considering the relationship between political theory and planning from a different, less orthodox angle.

NOTES

1. Jeremy Bentham, *A Fragment on Government* and *An Introduction to the Principles of Morals and Legislation* (ed. Wilfrid Harrison) (Oxford, Blackwell, 1960).
2. Ibid., p. 125.
3. A. J. Ayer, 'The Principle of Utility', in *Philosophical Essays* (London, Macmillan, 1954), pp. 250-70. Ayer's conclusion to this essay is very apt for my argument. It is that: '. . . while he did not succeed in setting either morals or politics "upon the sure path of a science", Bentham did produce a guide for action which it is possible to follow, though not perhaps exactly in the form in which he stated it' (p. 269).
4. S. K. Nath, *A Reappraisal of Welfare Economics* (London, Routledge 1969), p. 2, argues that: 'Though value-judgements are unavoidable in welfare economics, it is possible to try to pretend that any particular value-judgements adopted are so "widely acceptable", "general", or "minimal" that the welfare propositions based on them, would be quite general, non-controversial, or "more or less objective". This ideed has been the usual procedure in the literature of welfare economics.'
5. See J. R. Hicks, 'The Foundations of Welfare Economics', in *Economic Journal* (1939); J. R. Hicks, 'The Valuation of Social Income', in *Economica* (1940); N. Kaldor, 'Welfare Comparisons of Economics and Interpersonal Comparisons of Utility', in *Economic Journal* (1939).
6. S. H. Beer, *Modern British Politics* (London, Faber, 1965), p. xl.
7. W. J. M. Mackenzie, *Politics and Social Science* (Harmondsworth, Pelican, 1969), pp. 137-52.
8. Ibid., p. 144.
9. Ibid., p. 138.
10. Anthony Downs, *An Economic Theory of Democracy* (Harper & Row, 1957).
11. Reyner Banham, Paul Barker, Peter Hall, Cedric Price, 'Non-Plan: An Experiment in Freedom', in *New Society* (20 March 1969), pp. 435-44.
12. Peter Hall, 'The Great British History Parkway Drive-In', in *New Society* (3 March 1967), pp. 151-5.
13. Peter Hall, 'Roskill's Felicific Calculus', in *New Society* (19 February 1970), p. 306.
14. Peter Self, ' "Nonsense on Stilts": Cost-Benefit Analysis and the Roskill Commission', in *Political Quarterly*, Vol. 41 (1970), p. 251.

15. Department of the Environment, *Pedestrian Safety* (London, HMSO, 1973), p. 56.
16. Roy Gregory, *The Price of Amenity* (London, Macmillan, 1971), p. 26.
17. E. J. Mishan, *The Costs of Economic Growth* (Harmondsworth, Pelican, 1969), p. 193.
18. E. J. Mishan, 'The Spillover Enemy', in *Encounter*, Vol. 32 (1969), pp. 3-13.
19. E. J. Mishan, *Growth: The Price We Pay* (London, Staples, 1969).
20. Quoted by Jon Tinker, 'Ecology at the Hustings', in *New Scientist*, Vol. 46, No. 705 (1970), pp. 98-100.
21. Douglas Jay, 'The Cost of Urban Motorways', in *Town and Country Planning*, Vol. 38 (1970), pp. 98-100.
22. Self, op. cit., p. 256.

Chapter 8

Political Theory and Planning: Heterodox

The Benthamite liberal tradition represents one variety of political theory which has a relevance for planning, possibly the most important in its effects, but by no means the only one. By a political theory I mean a theory of man's nature and legitimate ends in society which is at least relevant to the question of how man ought to be governed.

One problem is that there are so many ambiguities in the Benthamite position that it becomes difficult to say what clearly falls outside permissible varieties of Benthamism. Within the main structure of the argument there can be diverse interpretations of what is to count as evidence that an individual has a preference, of the time-span over which we are going to maximise aggregate preferences, of how the value of a non-marketable good is to be treated. The consequence of this is that the basic structure of argument seems to be able to support practical conclusions which vary from Mishan to Hall. Radical criticisms of the existing ways in which decisions are made can be put forward from a Benthamite standard. I have one of my own: the Fallacy of the Active Want. It seems to me that in trying to evaluate the importance of environmental goods or situations, too much emphasis is placed on preferences which are expressed in action. This equation of evaluation with action occurs throughout the planning system, but an interesting example is to be found in the ways in which county planning authorities have tried to evaluate rural areas by measuring how many people go there, or how much people are prepared to spend in getting there. Lancashire have done this with the Forest of Bowland and Hampshire with the New Forest. The fallacy lies in thinking that the only kind of benefit men can get from anything must be from actually using it. But it seemes to me that this must always be an under-evaluation. When a thing is important to us, we get pleasure from it actually being there, without doing anything about it. I am glad the Forest of Bowland is

still beautiful—I would be hostile to any economic pressures put on it—
even though I have not found time to visit it for a matter of years. Just
as a man may love his parents though never get round to visiting them
or as a Londoner may count the Theatre and Cinema of London among
his greatest assets as a source of pride and ever-present opportunities,
though he may scarcely ever visit them, so men love the physical being
of their country without necessarily doing anything about it.

We can best typify what constitutes an external, rather than an
internal, criticism of administrative Benthamism in logical terms. The
theoretical alternative is to have a prioristic theory of man which does
not regard any conclusion about man's ultimate or legitimate ends as
dependent on evidence about men's behaviour or preferences. In
Mackenzie's account of political economy he emphasises that the
protagonists have always insisted that maximisation (of the collective
entity) relates to individuals in the here and now and not some abstract
entity as *volk*, state or nation. This is most clear in Bergson's 'fundamental value premise'. Nor must it be composed of conceptions of man
other than he is: man cannot have drives which he is not conscious of,
nor can he be part of a tradition which runs counter to his present
desires.

THE IMPORTANCE OF J. S. MILL

John Stuart Mill is often thought of as Utilitarian, but consistently in
his writings we find stressed the idea of important values not served by
the principle of utility and capable of being in direct opposition to it.
In 'Utilitarianism' he insisted that the quality of pleasures was important, notwithstanding the quantity. Some pleasures are 'higher' than
others and: 'It is better to be a human being dissatisfied than a pig
satisfied; better to be Socrates dissatisfied than a fool satisfied. And if
the fool, or the pig, are of a different opinion, it is because they only
know their own side of the question. The other party to the comparison
knows both sides.'[1]

Mill's 1838 essay on 'Bentham', though starting as an almost
reverential obituary and giving Bentham credit for many achievements,
culminates in a fundamental attack on the consequences of Bentham
principle:

'If Bentham's theory of life can do so little for the individual, what can
it do for society?

'It will enable a society which has attained a certain state of spiritual
development, and the maintenance of which in that state is otherwise
provided for, to prescribe the rules by which it may protect its material
interests. It will do nothing (except sometimes as an instrument in the

hands of a higher doctrine) for the spiritual interests of society; nor does it suffice of itself even for the material interests. That which alone causes any material interests to exist, which alone enables any body of human beings to exist as a society, is national character: *that* it is, which causes one nation to succeed in what it attempts, another to fail; one nation to understand and aspire to elevated things, another to grovel in mean ones; which makes the greatness of one nation lasting, and dooms another to early and rapid decay. The true teacher of the fitting social arrangements for England, France or America, is the one who can point out how the English, French or American character can be improved, and how it has been made what it is.'[2]

As a fundamental objection to Bentham, this is clear enough and it has implications for any theory of planning. But in *The Principles of Political Economy*, Mill's attitude to what we now call 'environmental' questions is more explicit. This is particularly so in Book IV, Chapter 6, which is entitled 'Of the Stationary State'. In effect, this chapter is an attack on the value of economic growth; the conventional belief, by political economists of the period, that well-being must always consist in expanding wealth and capital:

'I cannot, therefore, regard the stationary state of capital and wealth with the unaffected aversion so generally manifested towards it by political economists of the old school. I am inclined to believe that it would be, on the whole, a very considerable improvement on our present condition. I confess I am not charmed with the ideal of life held out by those who think that the normal state of human beings is that of struggling to get on; that the trampling, crushing, elbowing and treading on each other's heels, which form the existing type of social life, are the most desirable lot of human kind, or anything but the disagreeable symptoms of one of the phases of industrial progress . . . the best state for human nature is that in which, while no one is poor, no one desires to be richer, nor has any reason to fear being thrust back, by the efforts of others to push themselves forward.'[3]

I find this passage astonishingly modern as social criticism; apart from the Victorian style, one could easily believe that it was written in the late sixties of this century. This impression of contemporaneity is heightened when Mill goes on to discuss the question of population growth:

'There is room in the world, no doubt, and even in old countries, for a great increase of population, supposing the arts of life to go on improving, and capital to increase. But even if innocuous, I confess I see very little reason for desiring it. The density of population necessary to enable mankind to obtain, in the greatest degree, all the advantages both of co-operation and of social intercourse, has, in all the most populous countries been attained. A population may be too crowded, though all be amply supplied with food and raiment. It is not good for man to be kept perforce at all times in the presence of his species. A world from which solitude is extirpated, is a very poor ideal. Solitude, in the sense of being often alone, is essential to any depth of meditation or of character; and solitude in the presence of natural beauty and grandeur, is the cradle of thoughts and aspirations which are not only good for the individual, but which society could ill do without. Nor is there much satisfaction in contemplating the world with nothing left to the spontaneous activity of nature; with every rood of land brought into cultivation, which is capable of growing food for human beings; every flowery waste or natural posture ploughed up, all quadrupeds or birds which are not domesticated for man's use exterminated as his rivals for food, every hedgerow or superfluous tree rooted out, and scarcely a place left where a wild shrub or flower could grow without being eradicated as a weed in the name of improved agriculture. If the earth must lose that great portion of its pleasantness which it owes to things that the unlimited increase of wealth or population would extirpate from it, for the mere purpose of enabling it to support a larger, but not a better or a happier population, I sincerely hope, for the sake of posterity, that they will be content to be stationary, long before necessity compels them to it.'[4]

Mill, then, is the unrecognised mentor of the modern, radical conservationist who combines his love of the natural environment with a distaste for the competitive and acquisitive society which threatens to destroy it. In his love of the countryside, as in his rejection of the Benthamite technique for evaluating its worth, he is splendidly relevant to the planning problems of the 1970s.

THE NAZI LAW OF 1935

Nazism and Fascism both involve prioristic theories of man's nature (however crude) and the equation of a man's interests with an idealised and abstracted concept of the man as member of a race or nation. For this reason both are opposed to the Benthamite principle of life and both involve the consideration of aggregates, not as reducible to individuals, but as having separate needs and existence of their own: the race, the *volk*, the nation. This has an application to the environment which can be seen most clearly in the *Reichsnaturschutzgesetz* law of 26 June 1935. The preamble to this legislation states:

'Today as formerly nature in wood and field is the object of the desire, the joy and the recreation of the German people.

'The landscape of the countryside has however been completely changed in these latter years, its garb of trees and flowers owing to intensive agriculture and aforestation, to narrow minded cleaning up of meadows and to the cultivation of conifers has been in many places completely altered. Many species of animals which inhabited wood and field have disappeared with the disappearance of their natural haunts.

'While such developments were often an economic necessity, we are today conscious of the ideal as well as of the economic damage wrought by such mass transformation.

'The protection of objects of natural interest (*Naturdenkmalpflege*) which has been growing for centuries could be carried out with but partial success, because the necessary political and cultural conditions were lacking. It was only the transformation of the German man which created the preliminary conditions necessary for an effective system of protection of Natural Beauty.

'The Government of the German Realm considering it to be its duty to preserve for the poorest members of the people their share in the natural beauties of the German scene has therefore decided to enact the following law for the protection of natural beauties which is hereby made public.'[5]

The law then goes on to lay down procedures and authorities for the preservation of monuments, animals, plant life and special areas—much as a combination of British laws does now, but in a vastly different legal and administrative structure. In the language of the preamble we can see some of the more important contrasts with Benthamism: the 'ideal' is contrasted with the 'economic'; agricultural progress is 'narrow-minded'; it required the 'transformation of German man' before conservation could take place. One hopes that conservation is in no way stigmatised—as many social practices have been—by its association with Nazism. In Nazi lore, of course, the countryside carried special connotations of 'Nature' with a capital 'N' and of wholesome German innocence.

It is important, too, to note Section 8 (1) (c) which lays down procedures for 'The education of public opinion in regard to the necessity of protecting the beauties of Nature'. Perhaps I am reading too much into a nuance, but it seems to me that the logic is reversed here: opinion is to be created by policy; policy is not the consequence of demand.

ENVIRONMENTAL TROTSKYISM

In Marxism, too, existing opinion or demand in a corrupt society is devalued. Criticising Feuerbach, Marx stipulated that 'the essence of man is not an abstraction inherent in each single individual. The real nature of man is the totality of social relations.'[6]

This was with reference to the understanding of religious belief and institutions, but the approach has clear implications for the treatment of environmental problems. As revolutionary historical development changes the nature of man's social relations, we would expect that the relation between man and environment would also change. Briefly, existing human beliefs about, and interests in, the environment are irrelevant, for in a post-revolutionary situation man will come to look upon the environment as common and have a wider awareness of its development potential and of his own control of it for his own, un-alienated purposes. Subsequent 'Marxism' has not emphasised these implications—on the whole it has had more urgent preoccupations—but Trotsky saw them clearly:

'Through the machine man in socialist society will command nature in its entirety, with its grouse and its sturgeons. He will point out places for mountains and for passes. He will change the course of rivers, and he will lay down rules for the oceans. The idealist simpletons may say that this will be a bore, but that is why they are simpletons. Of course, this does not mean that the entire globe will be marked off into boxes, that the forests will be turned into parks and gardens. Most likely, thickets and forests and grouse and tigers will remain.

'And man will do it so well that the tiger won't even notice the machine, or feel the change, but will live as he lived in primeval times. The machine is not in opposition to the earth. The machine is the instrument of man in every field of life.'[7]

Trotsky's imagination places us in a world far removed from that of the moderate Benthamites. Policy decisions are hardly relevant here. It is a mistake to ask: 'How does one choose between revolutionary new environments? How does one plan them?'

The belief in a new Socialist man in a new Socialist environment is by no means dead. It is still to be found on the fringes of the planning literature. For instance Maurice Ash, in his essay 'The Environment Business'[8] in the *Town and Country Planning* issue of the same name, criticised the participants in the London Ringway controversy for asking the wrong, unimaginative questions. '. . . The city must die to be reborn in some quite different guise', he concludes. Contemporary planning of the rural environment he dismisses as 'preserving middle-class interests' which is, at least, a frank statement of a common assumption.

There is a strange, if superficial, similarity in this approach to the 'Non-Plan' visions of Professor Hall *et al.* I for one do not find this surprising.

ENVIRONMENTAL ROUSSEAUISM

Rousseau, too, is associated in the history of political ideas with precisely the approach to social decisions that liberal economists and administrators have rejected: viz. the maximisation of some collective entity not reducible to individuals. One expression of this approach in *The Social Contract* is: 'the general will is always right and tends to the public advantage; but it does not follow from this that the deliberations of the people are always equally correct. Our will is always for our own good, but we do not always see what that is. . . .'[9]

In the history of literary images, Rousseau is thought of as a romantic and Romanticism (though a vague concept or movement at best) is seen as the beginning of modern man's extolment and pursuit of rural tranquillity. These associations are borne out by some of Rousseau's writings. Take, for instance, this passage from the confessions:

'I like to walk at my leisure and halt when I please. The wandering life is what I like. To journey on foot, unhurried, in fine weather and in fine country, and to have something pleasant to look forward to at my goal, that is of all ways of life the one that suits me best.

'It is already clear what I mean by fine country. Never does a plain, however beautiful it may be, seem so in my eyes. I need torrents, rocks, firs, dark woods, mountains, steep roads to climb or descend, abysses beside me to make me afraid.'[10]

Combining these two strands of Rousseau's thought we can form a general approach to environmental problems and policy. It is this: a 'natural' and attractive rural environment where man can wander freely is a necessary condition of the general happiness and ought to be preserved (or allowed to redevelop if necessary) without regard to the self-perceived interests of the citizens.

Like environmental Trotskyism, this approach lies on the fringes of contemporary debate. Something very similar to it is to be found in some Fabian writings and in some of the propaganda of the amenity societies. To find such an approach in government circles one must go back to the 1940s. A clear instance is the Scott Committee on Land Utilisation in Rural Areas, which reported in 1942. 'We have become convinced', the Committee wrote in its Introduction, 'if we were not before, that there is an innate love of nature deeply planted in the heart of man. Indeed, our views have been beautifully stated by G. M. Trevelyan: "Without vision the people perish, and without natural beauty the English people will perish in the spiritual sense." '

This document is still the cornerstone of British recreational planning. It is paradoxical that its views would now be considered dogmatic and sentimental by many planners.

ENVIRONMENTAL HIGH TORYISM

In many respects both the arguments and the policy recommendations of environmental High Toryism are similar to those of Rousseauism. Both stress the need for, and duty of, preservation without reference to social class, conflicting interests or popular wishes. But there is a fundamental difference: whereas the Rousseauist bases his argument on 'human need' (that is, biology), the Tory bases his arguments on cultural phenomena, on the specialness of the English 'heritage'. It is reminiscent, in some ways, of Burke's approval of the Parliament's action in claiming its rights from Charles I: '. . . not on abstract principles as the rights of man, but as the rights of Englishmen, and as a patrimony derived from their forefathers.'[11]

One example of this approach is to be found in a talk given by Lt-Col. Gerald Haythornthwaite, an official of the CPRE in Yorkshire, entitled, 'My Case for Preservation'. [12] 'Our consciousness is ancient', he argues, 'and we need to feel our roots and be reminded of our history.' He goes on: 'We are the recipients of a glorious heritage of buildings and landscape not contrived on the cheap in response to popular clamour, but raised up, without considering cost, to the glory of God and mankind, and it is up to us to leave behind as large a slice as possible of our inherited riches.'

The insistence on culturally imposed duties of preservation is often almost a *bête noire* of modern planning. The amenity societies, including the CPRE, studiously avoid it when they participate in public controversy, preferring to put their case within the Benthamite framework. But that is not to say that they and, for that matter, many planners, do not believe it as private individuals outside the context of public argument.

CONCLUSION: CONSERVATION AS AN END

I have been concerned in this chapter to show how conservation can be argued as an end without reference to Benthamite notions of goals, wants, preferences, and the like. There are ways, too, in which anti-conservation can be argued as an end (the Italian 'Futurist' movement would furnish some interesting examples), but these are less common. I am certainly not arguing that Benthamism is anti-conservationist. Indeed, footnote 16 of Chapter 5 of *Principles of Morals and Legislation* is a classification of the 'pleasures of the country scene'. But Benthamism is not essentially conservationist; it is neutral. And all the arguments in this chapter are conservationist theories either in the sense that they allow for fundamental evaluations without reference to the states of mind of existing people or in the sense that they specifically argue the intrinsic value of the environment, or both. John Stuart Mill is the clearest case, because he does both and connects the two arguments.

Love of the countryside, resentment and fear of development have been emotions shared by many intellectuals in the past century and are half regardless of whether they are 'left', 'right', 'centre' or just eccentric. But it is worth remembering that the countryside was not always valued so highly before industrial forms of life began to predominate. Consider the urbane and unromantic Sydney Smith's description of a journey through the Gloucestershire Cotswolds:

'. . . one of the most unfortunate and desolate counties under heaven, divided by stone walls, and abandoned to the screaming kites and larcenous crows: after travelling really twenty, and to appearance ninety, miles over this region of stone and sorrow, life begins to be a burden, and you wish to perish.'[13]

NOTES

1. John Stuart Mill, 'Utilitarianism', in *Utilitarianism*, ed. Mary Warnock (Glasgow, Fontana, 1962), p. 260.
2. John Stuart Mill, 'Bentham', in ibid., p. 105.
3. John Stuart Mill, *Collected Works*, Vol. 3 (London and Toronto, Routledge, 1965), pp. 753-4.
4. Ibid., p. 765.
5. Quoted in Lord Howard of Penrith, 'Lessons from Other Countries', in Clough Williams-Ellis (ed.), *Britain and the Beast* (Readers' Union by arrangement with J. M. Dent, 1938).
6. 'Theses on Feuerbach', Vol. 6, in T. B. Bottomore and Maximilian Rubel, *Karl Marx: Selected Writings in Sociology and Social Philosophy*, (Hardmondsworth, Penguin, 1965), p. 83.
7. L. Trotsky, 'Revolutionary and Socialist Art', in *Literature and Revolution* (Michigan, 1966), p. 252.
8. Maurice Ash, 'The Environment Business', in *Town and Country Planning*, Vol. 28 (March 1970), pp. 143-6.
9. J. J. Rousseau, *The Social Contract* (London, Everyman, 1966), p. 22.
10. J. J. Rousseau, *The Confessions* (Harmondsworth, Penguin, 1966), p. 167.
11. Edmund Burke, *Reflections on the Revolution in France* (Harmondsworth, Penguin, 1969), p. 118.
12. Gerald Haythornthwaite, 'My Case for Preservation', in *The Listener* (24 February 1966).
13. Quoted in A. E. Trueman, *Geology and Scenery in England and Wales* (London, Penguin, 1949), p. 14.

Chapter 9

'Participation' in the Planning Process

'Participation' has become a vogue word in recent years, both in discussions of planning and in academic political theory. In political theory the vogue can be seen as the partial rejection of what has been called 'the élitist theory of democracy' developed by Joseph Schumpeter in the 1940s. According to Schumpeter, the definition of democracy relevant to modern industrial societies was: 'that institutional arrangement for arriving at political decisions, in which individuals acquire the power to decide by means of a competitive struggle for the people's vote'.[1]

Schumpeter claimed that this definition provided a distinction between democracies and other forms of government which was realistic in that it acknowledged the necessity of leadership, the existence of power, and the essentially negative role of the ordinary citizen in the running of the state. For perhaps twenty-five years the mainstream of democratic theory, especially in Britain and America, developed within Schumpeter's framework. The more distinguished developments included Anthony Downs's 'Economic Theory of Democracy',[2] Robert Dahl's theory of 'Polyarchy',[3] and Bernard Crick's concept of politics in his book *In Defence of Politics*.[4] But, since the mid-1960s, this framework has been increasingly under attack by writers claiming that Schumpeter's 'democracy' was not necessarily democracy at all, and was certainly not the highest political aspiration for modern societies. Among the more distinguished books of this phase are Peter Bachrach's *The Theory of Democratic Elitism*[5] and Carole Pateman's *Participation and Democratic Theory*.[6] Necessarily, to attack Schumpeter is to prescribe a more positive role for the ordinary citizen in the running of the state and thus to talk about participation. Concepts of participation have entered a number of areas of argument during this period: academic political theory, industrial relations, 'community' politics, and the British planning process.[7]

G

Why the change of emphasis? In my view, the pressure came from ordinary citizens themselves. Schumpeter's definition was acceptable so long as the 'democracies' it defined (Britain, parts of Western Europe, North America, and the 'white' dominions of the British Commonwealth) were stable and successful. But by the end of the 1960s, they were no longer so stable; it became clear that many citizens in America, in Britain and in France were no longer satisfied with their role. Participation theory was largely the effect, not the cause, of this change.

THE AMBIGUITIES OF PARTICIPATION

There is a grave problem of meaning about the word 'participation' not often appreciated by those who argue about it. At the simplest level, as Aldous and others have pointed out, participation is often confused with complaints about the lack of (opportunities for) participation.[8] Clearly 'participation' in the context of arguments about planning and politics means political action, and increases and decreases in the level of participation, in one dimension, are increases and decreases in the number of citizens who are politically active. But by saying this we have solved few problems and created many. To what extent must participation be efficacious? Or does the ineffective pressure group or political sect, whose members may in an obvious sense be more politically active than their apathetic fellow-citizens, count as participation? In some cases, of course, political action may have results which change a situation in the opposite direction to that which the 'participant' intended. Can we count a level of participation as low where we find an absence of widespread political activity but at the same time the general lines of policy seem quite conducive to the balance of interests and values in the community? This situation could occur in two ways; either because of the efficacity of public opinion as a potential (though unrealised) sanction on public policy or merely because of the Utilitarian norms of politicians and administrators. Yet in some ways these constitute a substitute for participation rather than participation itself.

Let us consider the following criteria of participation:

1. The number of citizens acting politically.
2. The amount of their action.
3. The overall effect of their action on policy.
4. The conformance of policies to the preferences of political actors.
5. The conformance of policies to the preferences of all citizens.
6. The preferences of citizens as a causal factor in the production of policies.

Let us assume the impossible: that these are variables which can be quantified. After all, we would in ordinary language talk about 'greater' or 'lesser' degrees of them as we would of participation itself. A moment's consideration could assure us that they at least vary independently and in many cases there will be an inverse relation between two variables. This will occur for instance, when an organised minority (defined in terms of preferences) moves into action. 1-4 may go up and 5 and 6 down. Or, if they are a total failure, 1-3 may go up, 4 down, while 5 and 6 remain the same.

Participation is a failure as a concept because of this systematic ambiguity. Once we agree that we are going to allow only efficacious participation to count (and otherwise we have no way of excluding the man who reiterates Hitler's speeches day after day in the asylum) then it becomes clear that for many cases it is not possible to say what is to count as an increase in participation.

These are massive reservations to any concept of participation but they do not apply to every case. Participation remains a meaningful concept, and an admirable ideal, for at least the limiting case where all six variables can be increased together. That is, we can talk unreservedly about participation where increasing political action by citizens, representing the true balance of preferences in the political unit, leads to a greater conformance of policies to citizens' wishes. Even so, three major forms of participation can be distinguished.

(a) 'Public' participation as a right of all citizens to be involved in policy-forming processes.
(b) 'Pressure' participation as the practice of organised groups of citizens of attempting to influence the policy-forming process.
(c) 'Passive' participation as a general public awareness of issues which, by its very existence, modifies the policy-forming process.

Most of the attempts, like those of the Skeffington Committee, to prescribe increases in participation involve all three forms, though they often distinguish between the first two.

WHY PARTICIPATION?

'Participation', as a word, has taken on some of the mantle of 'democracy'. It is a good thing. It has what C. L. Stevenson would have called a 'dynamic emotive meaning'.[9] If it is a good thing, it can only be so for two reasons; either as an end in itself or as a method for producing 'better' decisions. There are two separate ways of claiming participation as an end even where it might produce 'worse' decisions (though this is not a common admission). Participation is arguable in terms of democracy as a political value or in terms of its role in political education. Both democracy and education have a claim to be considered primary social goals.

The claim of participation as a method is even more diversified, for the 'quality' of a decision can be argued in many ways. At one level it has a mundane, even sordid, meaning for administrators: a less troublesome decision. Sir Colin Buchanan, for instance, said in an interview with Tony Aldous in *The Times* that he had formed his opposition to Cublington Airport despite the technical 'evidence' produced by the economists not only on environmental grounds but also because, politically, he 'smelt trouble'.[10] The same attitude was taken by the Ministry Inspector at the Inquiry into the Holme Pierrepoint power station who according to Gregory felt that the site was objectively the right one, but too politically dangerous.[11] Of course, one could justify the administrator's search for convenience into a political theory. For instance, within the framework of Bernard Crick's *In Defence of Politics* it could be argued that the ability of certain groups to cause trouble and therefore get their own way may not produce good results in itself but it is part of an overall form of social organisation, politics, which is superior to all other overall forms of social organisation. A similar case has often been put for capitalism: that its particular effects might be replaceable by better, but only at the cost of endangering capitalism as a system, and that as an overall system of economic organisation it is superior to its rivals.

A stronger theoretical claim is that increasing levels of participation increases levels of utility by more effectively channelling preferences (possibly sifted in terms of their intensity) into decision-making. This argument falls clearly into a framework with which we are already familiar; the Utilitarian tradition. Again, there is a parallel argument for capitalism as a consistent and necessary maximiser of utilities, as in Marshall's analysis of perfect competition.

Finally, increasing participation can 'improve' decisions in a less theoretical way by maximising the detail of information assumed by the decision. 'Only the wearer knows where the shoe pinches'; in this sense, only by allowing participation can the full practical implications of a policy be grasped. This, of course, is a claim which can be made quite independent of the first two.

THE APPLICATION TO PLANNING

Aldous poses a more specific set of arguments for participation in the planning process. In many ways they simply reinforce the general arguments for participation. The argument from avoiding trouble is made particular:

'. . . on a crudely practical level, belated awareness of what is proposed can cause more trouble from a public opinion which thinks it has been misled or kept in the dark, than explaining, listening and modifying early on. The explosion of wrath from a public which thinks it has been duped, and the often quite skilful and resourceful campaign of opposition it may put up in the press and at the public inquiry which then becomes necessary is a price less and less worth paying to avoid the initial trouble, time and expense of early, adequate, public consultation'[12]

Participation is necessary because of the importance of the planning process. Aldous says that 'the physical planning process concerns us all in a very thorough-going and permanent way'.[13] Or again: 'A planning decision these days can sometimes have a greater effect on the life of an individual than a prison sentence—and certainly on an individual as a member of a community.'[14] It must be 'direct' because of the inadequacies of the normal channels of communication between decision-makers and public when it comes to environmental issues. 'If all councillors—or even a sizeable proportion of them—were elected on an environmental ticket after election campaigns in which planning questions played a prominent part, there might be less need for "participation".'[15]

Moreover, participation can improve planning in a way which overlaps with my final general justification, by leading opinion. 'The environmentally aware view tends to be one which is ahead of public opinion and ahead of council chamber opinion—but which does become accepted later.'[16]

Taking these last two points together, it becomes clear that Mr Aldous is talking only, or at least very largely, about a very limited form of participation, roughly equivalent to my category of 'pluralist' participation. Indeed, he partially admits this when saying: 'The spearhead of public participation has been, and increasingly will be, the amenity societies.'[17] The last statement is only an admission of what inevitably follows from what has been said so far. For if participation is to concern itself with issues which do not trouble the electorate, *qua* electorate, and if it is expected to be 'ahead' of both public opinion and decision-makers' opinion, it cannot be mass participation. The question remains as to whether it can be representative. The sort of participation Aldous in practice recommends (active groups) is scarcely justifiable in terms of the strongest theoretical claim for participation (that it serves as a maximiser of utilities). Indeed, it has often been argued that amenity groups are not representative of public opinion, usually because they are middle-class. Concessions to this argument have been made by a number of ministers, including Mr Crosland and Mr Walker. More virulently, Mr William Small has attacked the Conservation Society (in the January 1967 issue of *Town and Country Planning*):

'Paraphrased, the objectives of these people should be stated thus, "There are too many of the wrong kind of people in this country. Those who ride and shoot and fish trout and play golf and live at densities of one family to every ten acres are O.K. and we want to make sure that they don't have their style cramped by trespassers. But picnickers, hikers, or artisans with ambitions to own semi-detacheds, owners of small family saloons and weekend seaside trippers are proliferating dangerously. So let's make sure they don't get out of hand".'[18]

Mr Aldous at least has the courage to face up to this argument, which can often be the most embarrassing to conservationists for it makes them appear not at the front line of an existing participatory democracy, but as one of the obstacles to a potential participatory democracy. In a section entitled 'Conservation and Class',[19] he asserts the counter-claim as follows: 'In an increasing number of cases, the "selfish", "middle-class" accusation seems to be thrown in simply to bolster anti-conservation arguments which are themselves selfish and sectional. This is unfortunate because it obscures the real issues and tends to devalue the language of conservation.' The language used here, as elsewhere, hints of commitment, but in the end Aldous ducks the issue by asserting the unreality of the conflict. It is unreal partly because economic prosperity is a necessary condition of environmental control (an argument I find more convenient than convincing when applied to particular issues) and partly because of the potential of 'environmental education', presumably to change the nature of demand.

However, there are real issues, not simply conflicts of interest, but also conflicts of theory and principle. Suppose 'conservation' is a middle-class preference to which the working class is hostile or apathetic. This itself is a mighty supposition. It depends on an adequate concept of class which correlates with consistent opposition to conservation among the working class. A great deal has been done, academically, to satisfy the first condition, but with only limited success, and little if anything to satisfy the second. But even if the assumption is made, there remains a range of arguments which might justify conservation as being in the general interest.

1. *The representative élite argument.* Rather as John Stuart Mill saw the middle classes as the guardians of culture and individuality (in general, what was valuable in a society), it could be argued that the middle-class conservationists are the protectors of what is valuable in the environment. Not that the benefits are specific to the middle class, but the intelligence and information required to understand the nature of the benefits is concentrated in the middle class.

2. *The embourgeoisement thesis.* Social change is eradicating many essential features of the working class as a class in a process which is

essentially one of increasing numbers of people becoming middle-class. Therefore middle-class preferences are a better guide to future working-class preferences than are present working-class preferences.

3. *The 'natural man' argument.* We have already seen that there can be *a priori* arguments about human interests. Here, the case would again be that there is something natural and of permanent value to man in the benefits which conservation seeks to preserve and development to destroy. For some reason, perhaps connected with education or economic opportunities, the middle classes are aware of their nature and the working classes misunderstand their (identical) nature.

4. *The argument from intensity.* A long, primarily American tradition of democratic theory ranging from Madison and Jay in the eighteenth century to Dahl and Poliby in our own times, has asserted that simple majorities cannot be regarded as definitive of correct policies. We need to take into account intensities—the level at which citizens care about the difference between two policies. In its clearest case, the argument from intensity justifies the political victory of an intense minority over a majority whose policy-preference is more marginal. In constitutional terms, this lends its support to complex rather than simple procedures. The application to planning is easy: the open competition of pressure groups for support from the public and influence on the policy process is, arguably, the best realistic method of filtering political action for its intensity. Limited participation can thus be superior, in Utilitarian terms, to artificially stimulated mass participation.

It is worth following the argument so far back into its premises to see in perspective the theoretical dimension of the controversy. But in the end, it scarcely matters. There is no convincing evidence of a coherent working-class opposition to conservation. The prevailing working-class attitude is probably the same as the prevailing middle-class attitude: defensive towards amenities apparent and available to them, acquisitive towards developments beneficial to them, and completely unaware of the contradictions of this approach considered aggregatively.

THE SKEFFINGTON REPORT: INTERPRETING
PARTICIPATION IN PRACTICE

As I have implied, the Skeffington Report[20] was a rather nebulous document; 'trendy but toothless' is one trite but fair assessment. The report, published in 1969, was set up to define more precisely the form that should be taken by participatory machinery necessary in view of the requirement of local planning authorities under the 1968 Town and Country Planning Act to consult the public on structure and local plans.

But it falls very far short of precise definitions. Very little of what is said in the nine recommendations is not extremely basic. By that I mean that it follows from a minimal definition of participation and a little common sense. The public are to be given information (I) and information about the availability of information (II). In a long planning process there is a need for continuous representations, though the stage after the formulation of options and the stage after the formulation of proposals are especially crucial (III). Information should be provided in the areas to which it is relevant and people should be told what, if anything, they have achieved by participation (VII). Citizens should be advised to assist with, as well as to express views on, the planning process (VIII). The need for 'better knowledge' is reiterated (IX). Only recommendations IV and VI can in fact be described as proposals. They are, respectively, the establishment of community forums to co-ordinate public interest in planning and the appointment of community development officers to 'secure the involvement of those people who do not join organisations'. Both were specifically rejected by a Department of Environment circular of late 1970:[21] 'The Secretaries of State are of the opinion expressed by a number of the organisations consulted on the Report, that neither community forums nor the appointment of community development officers will prove to be necessary in the specific context of development plans.'

The other recommendations are not rejected (indeed it would be difficult and unnecessary to reject any prescriptions as nebulous as these), but they are minimally interpreted. For example:

(On information) 'This does not mean an unending flow of information which would inevitably make unreasonable demands on resources and in the end defeat its own object.'
(On alternative structure plans) 'Only realistic alternatives should be published and where the local planning authorities have a clear preference they should indicate this.'
(On public assistance with tasks of planning) 'This could prove a useful way of involving the public provided authorities ensure that people are not asked to do work for which they are not equipped.'

In effect, the circular interpreted what was, anyway, a fairly minimal or ambiguous concept of participation almost down to the status of a formality or dignified element. But one might well ask what else it could do. Any genuine attempt to increase all the major participation variables (numbers, average time spent, the sum of effect induced on decisions by the public) raises some enormous problems of which the Skeffington Committee were, on the whole, aware. These can be summarised as follows.

1. *The theoretical weakness of the case for increasing participation; in that it is clear that participation can only be increased from a very low level to a slightly higher level.*[22] Mass participation is not in line with the sociological facts of life; nor could the system take the strain. At this realistic level there is absolutely no guarantee, as we have seen, that marginal increases in the participation variables have any positive effect on public welfare. Indeed, they may have a negative effect, as the Committee acknowledged in discussing pressure groups in Paragraph 92. Much as they admire the amenity societies: 'we think that it would be wrong to give statutory recognition to any organisation which represents only one of the multiplicity of interests affected by a plan'. Realistically, public assistance with the tasks of planning means the Warwickshire Women's Institute conducting a tree survey for the Warwickshire Planning Authority.

2. *The existing complexity of the planning process.* As we have seen, the production of structure plans and development plans is a lengthy process. Already the length of the process threatens to detract from its usefulness. As the Committee admit: 'In making our recommendations we have borne in mind that procedures for public participation have to be superimposed in what are already complex planning procedures.' Too real a sense of participation might make planning unworkable.

3. *The inherent lack of information.* However effective the 'variety of methods' (the Committee's phrase, recommendation I) used for communication, the public can never be sufficiently informed to participate fully for two reasons. Firstly, because people, who are usually busy or politically apathetic or both, cannot be changed quite so rapidly. Secondly, because the public could never be as informed as the planners unless they did the planners' job.

I regard this last problem as the least important of the three. As I have argued, planning is a political and not a technical exercise and the ability to make political value-judgements does not require the same degree of information as the translation of those judgements into practical policies. As a citizen, I can quite validly prefer a country with a stationary population, a minimal rate of urbanisation, and a large degree of preservation to its opposite without requiring detailed economic, demographic or architectural knowledge. As a teacher at the University of Warwick I find it easier to judge what I think is the right way for the University to develop (in aggregate numbers and general shape) than I do to deal with the far 'smaller' problem of what effect our current policy on admissions will have on our intake next year. The ability to make valid political judgements is, by its very nature, more widespread than the ability to make correct technical calculations.

So far I have looked at participation in terms of its conceptual ambiguities, the advantages of unambiguous participation, and the particular problems of participation in the planning process. Much of what might be called the case against participation is contained within the statement of these problems. An increase in participation can lead to a greater distortion of preferences, can overburden the planning system, or can result in a victory of ignorance over knowledge. We have seen already that the range of opportunities for the private citizen to involve himself in the planning process which has existed since 1947 has largely excited responses which are self-interested in the narrowest sense apart from those by organised attitude groups. In short, it is dubious whether the possible Utilitarian advantages of participation could justify adding further complexity to an already cumbersome planning process.

MODESTLY USEFUL PARTICIPATION

My scepticism about the meaning of participation and, where the meaning is clear, the value, does not imply that I reject participation. Indeed, there have been efforts by local planning authorities since 1969 to implement the more modest recommendations of the Skeffington Committee. More public meetings have been held, even if they usually take the form of the authorities explaining the plan rather than discussing it. The relationship between planners and pressure groups appears to have become even closer and there have been examples of amenity societies and educational organisations helping with plans. In some cases, notably Suffolk, a range of plans has been publicised as alternatives. However, the attitude of many planners to these rituals is certainly that they are an irrelevant formal duty for themselves, a dignified element within the system.

Aldous stipulates two conditions for effective participation:

'(1) That it should be early enough in the planning process for the public to feel that there is a real chance of major changes if they are shown to be needed. . . .

'(2) That the choice is a real one, not just "take it or leave it".'[23]

These are sensible conditions but their fulfilment is exactly what would raise all the dangers of participation that I have already discussed. That is, where it is imagined that participation will have a radical effect on the planning process. However, it is probably usually thought that participation will have only a modest effect on outcomes: the ritual retains a mildly 'efficient' facet, in Bagehot's terms.

In the end, this is as much as participation can achieve. For, as I have argued, environmental issues are long-term issues and in the long term it matters only that good and coherent decisions are made, not how they are made.

NOTES

1. Joseph A. Schumpeter, *Capitalism, Socialism and Democracy* (London, Allen & Unwin, 1943), p. 269.
2. Anthony Downs, *An Economic Theory of Democracy* (Harper & Row, 1957).
3. Robert A. Dahl, *A Preface to Democratic Theory* (University of Chicago Press, 1956), pp. 63-89.
4. Bernard Crick, *In Defence of Politics* (London, Weidenfeld & Nicolson, 1962).
5. Peter Bachrach, *The Theory of Democratic Elitism* (Little, Brown & Company, 1967).
6. Carole Pateman, *Participation and Democratic Theory* (Cambridge, CUP, 1970).
7. The range of essays in G. Parry (ed.), *Participation in Politics* (Manchester, Manchester University Press, 1972), exemplify the 'participation' fashion.
8. Tony Aldous, *Battle for the Environment* (Glasgow, Fontana, 1972), p. 267.
9. See C. L. Stevenson, 'The Emotive Meaning of Ethical Terms', in *Mind* (1937); and C. L. Stevenson, 'Persuasive Definitions', in *Mind* (1938).
10. See Aldous, op. cit., p. 249.
11. R. Gregory, *The Price of Amenity* (London, Macmillan, 1971), pp. 124-6.
12. Aldous, op. cit., p. 268.
13. Ibid., p. 267.
14. Ibid., pp. 282-3.
15. Ibid., p. 268.
16. Ibid., loc. cit.
17. Ibid., loc. cit.
18. William Small, 'Semi-Detached View', in *Town and Country Planning*, Vol. 35, No. 1 (January 1967).
19. Aldous, op. cit., pp. 238-40.
20. Ministry of Housing and Local Government, *People and Planning* (London, HMSO, 1969).
21. I am grateful to the (anonymous) authors of 'The Participation Swindle' in *Community Action* (February 1971), for drawing attention to the circular.
22. An interesting example of the successful local pressure-group's view of participation is furnished by Mrs Elizabeth Coxon, Chairman of the King's Sutton Motorway Action Group. When the Department of Environment approved a route for the M40 which was half a mile further from King's Sutton than that originally proposed by the

Midland Road Construction Unit she said: 'This is a great victory. It proves that participation really does work, and that if you try hard enough and long enough you can win' (*Birmingham Post*, 22 December 1973).

23. Aldous, op. cit., p. 272.

Chapter 10

Pressure-group Strategies and Conservation

In this chapter I am going to examine the nature and importance of amenity societies and conservationist groups from the point of view of pressure-group theory. Primarily, I will deal with the Council for the Protection of Rural England as one of the oldest and best-established groups, though it will be necessary to refer to other organisations within the 'amenity lobby' in order to best understand the nature of the CPRE. I hope it will become clear that the two kinds of study have a lot to offer one another—that understanding conservation throws a great deal of light on the problems of classifying and assessing pressure groups and that established pressure-group analysis is equally illuminating when applied to conservationist organisations.

PRESSURE GROUPS

It seems characteristic of the study of politics that its terms and concepts remain or become ambiguous and controversial. Unlike 'ergs', 'volts' and 'elasticities' one can never merely use political terms; it always seems necessary to define or analyse them. This is even true of that relatively small proportion of political terminology which is 'purpose-built', developed within the modern study of politics, and 'pressure group' is no exception. At the most fundamental, for instance, Professor Finer treats 'pressure groups' as a category within 'interest groups'. Most of the other writers who use both terms argue for arranging them the other way round. There exist many definitions of pressure groups and many typologies of pressure groups. The problems of the assessment of a group's resources and the estimation of a group's importance have also been treated very differently. I shall take one definition of 'pressure group', improve it slightly, and then suggest a method of classification which involves some new terms and a more coherent basis than many previous attempts.

'The field of pressure groups' is equivalent, according to W. J. M. Mackenzie, to 'the field of organised groups possessing both formal structure and real common interests in so far as they influence the decisions of public bodies'.[1] For my purposes, three further qualifications should be added:

(a) The groups should actually intend to influence public bodies. This is so as to exclude, say, academic or scientific organisations which may inadvertently influence public bodies as a consequence of their work. These are essentially a different phenomenon.

(b) They should not themselves be public bodies; it seems confusing to call, for example, the Treasury a pressure group in British politics.

(c) They should not necessarily possess real common interests but either common interests or common values.

This last condition relates closely to the problem of classifying pressure groups. Typologies have been based on a wide range of variables including size, type of constitution, methods and social composition of membership. But the most useful term, if it can be made workable, is the nature of the common purpose for which the group exists. Some, of course, will turn out to involve alliances of different purposes. Some may turn out to have no common purpose at all; this would be an interesting category. Distinguishing between interests and principles as the two main kinds of common purpose would be particularly useful, partly because in ordinary language we want to make distinctions between selfish and altruistic motivation, but also because other important aspects of pressure-group analysis can only be seen in terms of some clarified notion of the group's purpose (assessing a group's achievements, for instance).

A distinction between interests and principles can be made, using B. M. Barry's classification of wants, which I referred to in Chapter 2. Interests are privately oriented wants, those not logically dependent on public benefits (that is, benefits to an indefinite number of people). Principles are publicly oriented wants, which cannot be made coherent without reference to an indefinite number of people. These can be divided into want-regarding principles of the liberal Benthamite variety which take people's wants as their criterion and ideal-regarding principles (non-Benthamite) which require some concept of benefits to people which is not dependent on their wants. Finally, an individual's interests need not consist in the actual satisfaction of wants; they could be furthered also by his accruing a greater general potential (such as money, status, education in some situations) for the satisfaction of any want.

In real political situations groups and individuals tend to argue their goals in terms of interests and both kinds of principle simultaneously. They also rationalise interests in terms of principles and ideal-regarding principles in terms of want-regarding principles. But that does not imply that we cannot, in analysing their activities, usefully distinguish which is primary. Here is a set of categories of pressure groups based on a distinction between those where interests are primary purposes and those where principles are primary.

1. *Interest groups*
   (*a*) Major economic interest groups: those organisations which represent broad production-based interests and corresponding to what are normally regarded as social classes. This includes the Trades Union Congress and the Confederation of British Industry.
   (*b*) Minor economic interest groups: representing narrower definitions of production-based interests. This includes most individual unions at least where they manifest what Lenin called 'mere trade union consciousness'. Also included will be many trades and professional associations and individual firms when they try to influence public bodies.
   (*c*) Non-financial interest groups: cases where the group has a definable interest which is not predominantly financial. Some local amenity groups will fall into this category, particularly where they count success as development being excluded from their own area, even though it consequently happens somewhere else. We can also include, for instance, the British Zionist Federation and the Royal National Institute for the Blind.

2. *Principle groups*
   (*d*) Programmatic groups: those which proselytise a broad set of social policies and (usually) justify them with general theories of social benefit and social organisation. The Fabians, the Bow Group, and the British Humanists Association are among this group. So, I shall argue, are the Conservation Society.
   (*e*) Promotional groups: those which are unified by belief in the benefits of a single, definable reform. The Anti-Corn League is the classic historical example; more recently the Abortion Law Reform Association is a case. They appear to have survived the 1967 Act to the extent that they failed to get their full recommendations.

(f) Emphasis groups: by these I mean groups whose aims do not conflict in any clear-cut way with widely held social goals or values but where the group is motivated by a belief in the importance of certain values or the need for vigilance about them. One of the features of an emphasis group is, therefore, that it is unlikely to have self-announced enemies—organised groups who actually declare that they are opponents. The NSPCC and RSPCA fall into this category. 'Shelter' is coming to resemble it and the AA, surprisingly, shows many features of emphasis groups. The CPRE is best treated as being of this type.

POTENTIAL PRESSURE AND EFFECTIVE PRESSURE

Two further problems of pressure-group theory are closely related in practice, but most be kept analytically distinct. On the one hand, in studying pressure groups we want to be able to assess their achievements, their effective pressure. On the other hand, we want to talk about groups' resources, their potential for pressure. These are two distinct things; groups with large resources can fail to use them properly, for instance, and we must be able to speculate on the possibility of a group being effective where one does not actually exist.

Group achievement, effective pressure, is a concept similar to 'power' and 'influence'. In principle we are interested in two main kinds of variable.

Firstly, the extent to which outcomes (policies, social events) would have been different if the group had not acted. This involves counter-factual conditionals—speculative statements about what would have happened, but did not. There is an ambiguity, here, between a number of interpretations of the question. Do we compare what actually happened with what might have happened if the group had been different, or had pursued different tactics? Or with what might have happened if the group had not existed in what Mackenzie calls an 'organised' form? Or are we comparing with the hypothetical situation in which there do not exist individuals sharing the common purpose of the group? Clearly, there is a range of concepts of 'group' in any particular case and anybody assessing a pressure group must say which facets are important.

Secondly, the extent to which the difference in outcome due to a group's activity is a difference more in conformance with the group's intentions or goals. Some group may produce counter-productive results in that their organisation, activity or existence affect outcomes, but adversely in terms of their purposes. It would be foolish to call this 'effective pressure'.

Neither of these variables can be treated, except in very simple cases, as precise, and statements about them will rarely admit of irrefutable proof. Nor can they be treated, even loosely, as functions of each other. There will be cases where group G1 seems to have had a large impact on policy outcomes, though in many respects not the impact it would have desired, while group G2 has had a 'smaller' total impact, but a high success rate. In such a case it would be purely arbitrary to compare G1 and G2 in terms of effective pressure.

GROUP RESOURCES

The potential for pressure can perhaps best be understood in terms of the different kinds of political resource which groups can have. As with pressure groups themselves, I intend to list a number of types of resources, divided into two main types—sanctional resources and non-sanctional resources. Sanctions involve the ability to gain compliance from policy-makers by threatening that those policy-makers will be made worse off in terms of overall goals than they would have been had they complied. A third factor, acting as a quantifier on all resources, will be the resources of countervailing groups.

TYPES OF SANCTION

1. *Sanctional resources*
   (a) Vote-swinging: where a group can pose the possibility of losing policy-makers' votes. The National Farmers Union, because of its high level of cohesion and important strategic position in certain constituencies, is said to have gained political advantages from its electoral situation. So has the Lord's Day Observance Society, in that its members have (in the period between March and June 1969, for instance) systematically threatened MPs that they would vote against them in the event of their supporting Sunday reform. During this period, a Gallup poll showed 69 per cent in favour of reform and 22 per cent against, but the difference in intensity of feeling was such that MPs had no evidence that they would lose votes except by supporting reform. So despite the evidence of (numerous but mild) public support, a Private Members' Bill in favour of reform was dropped.
   (b) Economic sanctions: where a group can affect the extent to which a Government can achieve economic goals. Trade unions of certain sorts have this capability, but it is a card which they are often (rightly) reluctant to play. The economic sanctions could affect them as much as anyone else, or the

H

tactic could prove counter-productive in terms of popular support.

(c) Policy-implementation: where a group can control the whole question of whether certain policies can be implemented at all. The Police Federation is in this position with respect to certain aspects of criminal law. The Association of University Teachers, perhaps could have the potential to control implementation of certain educational policies such as university expansion.

2. *Non-sanctional resources*

(a) Expertise: where information and experience which the group possesses is useful to the public body and therefore a 'trading' relationship develops between the private group and the public body. Also, where knowledge and experience support effectiveness in argument.

(b) Contacts: in cases where a group has established habitual communications with a public body its efficiency of expression will be far greater than that of groups which lack such contacts. It may also come to have useful advance knowledge of the public body's aims, information and alternatives.

(c) Prestige: some group spokesmen (Lord Birkett as Chairman of the CPRE, for instance) can have greater fame and status than those of the public body. The public body then has to treat them with a certain amount of caution.

(d) Cultural bias: public attitudes to a group and the moral worth of its purposes may be such that it is embarrassing to publicly oppose the group and possibly necessary to at least pretend to share some of its values.

(e) Quality of activist: the personal qualities—nous, appeal, intelligence and so on—of group activists can be very important.

(f) Finance: can be the main determinant of the ability or inability to pursue certain patterns of action.

3. *Countervailing pressures*. Resources, however well used, are not in themselves the determinants of outcomes; they must be related to the resources of countervailing pressures. The Lord's Day Observance Society and the Law Society are both examples of groups which have been disproportionately effective because of the weakness of their natural enemies. The former is a contingent situation: it just so happens that there has been no organised group in favour of Sunday reform. The latter seems to be almost a necessary situation: people are only

solicitors' clients once or twice in their lives and the clients have no further reason for unity.

CONSERVATION

Conservation is political or social action in defence of the physical environment and levels of social benefit determined by the state of that environment. Typically these benefits are hygienic, aesthetic or recreational. In the United States emphasis in the use of the word has been primarily on the hygienic aspects; in Great Britain aesthetic and recreational benefits have traditionally been the prime objects of 'conservation', though American usages and arguments have had an impact in recent years.

Properly, then, conservationist groups should primarily be principle groups. On the other hand, many of the eight hundred and more local amenity societies registered with the Civic Trust are primarily interest groups, existing to preserve a definable area and its population against development. This makes them radically different from a national body like the CPRE.

THE COUNCIL FOR THE PROTECTION OF RURAL ENGLAND[2]

Constitution. Formally, the CPRE is a federation of other groups, composed of constituent bodies and linked with affiliated bodies. The constituent bodies are represented by one or two members each on the General Committee. The General Committee elects an Executive Committee which supervises the work of the professional officials of the CPRE at central and local levels. In the country, the CPRE is organised into a field administration of forty branches. In short, it is a federation mainly of actively-based groups which acts in most day-to-day matters through a head office in London and a structure of local branches.

There are 53 constituent bodies electing a total of 104 representatives to the General Committee, which meets annually. Some of the constituent bodies are predictable supporters of the protection of rural England: the Commons, Open Spaces and Footpaths Preservation Society; the Ramblers Association; the Anglers Co-operative Association; the Pure Rivers Society. Some might be thought potential enemies, including the Automobile Association, the Caravan Club and the Institution of Electrical Engineers. Many of the professional associations relevant to planning are also members: the Institute of Landscape Architects; the Royal Institute of Chartered Surveyors; the Town and Country Planning Association and the Town Planning Institute. Some quasi-public bodies are members; these include the Civic Trust, the National Trust, the Rural District Councils Association and the Urban

District Councils Association. Anomalously, but perhaps typically, there are some constituent bodies which sound as if they ought to be only affiliated bodies: the Girl Guides Association, the Cambridge Preservation Society, the Oxford Preservation Trust.

Affiliation means little except a small subscription, the statement of a common interest, and a formalisation of contacts for when the CPRE and the affiliated body might act in conjunction. There are over 108 affiliated bodies, the majority of which are territorially based preservation societies (for instance, the Oxshott Heath Conservators, the Society of Sussex Downsmen). A minority are of a similar nature to the constituent bodies (the Historic Churches Preservation Trust, the Institute of Park and Recreation Administration). Seven public elected bodies are affiliated: four rural district councils, two urban district councils and Telscombe Parish Council. The affiliation of the Sidcup and Chislehurst Ladies' Circle No. 165 proves nothing except that there are more things in Heaven and Earth than some of us normally imagine.

In the Head Office, often referred to as 'Headquarters Group', the Chairman (Lord Kennet since 1972), the two Vice-Chairmen and the two Joint Honorary Treasurers are unpaid but fairly full-time. There are four full-time administrators, two administrative secretaries and two assistant secretaries who do the bulk of the work in the office.

There are forty CPRE branches, chiefly based on counties for the obvious reason that the local planning authorities which produce plans and deal with planning applications affecting most rural land are themselves based on counties. Most are called 'branches', though Kent has a 'Committee', Sussex a 'Joint Committee', Surrey an 'Amenity Council' and Suffolk a 'Preservation Society'. In the cases of Exmoor and the Peak District, branches are structured to deal with the Park Management Committee and the Park Planning Board respectively. Despite the anomalies, the general pattern is fairly uniform: the branches operate as smaller versions of the CPRE. Lancashire, for example, has a General Council representing local authorities and affiliated organisations which elects an Executive Committee. The Executive Committee is served by two full-time professional administrators. Money comes not just from the local authorities and affiliated organisations, but also from three categories of member-life, covenanted and subscriber. Lancashire is exceptional in its employment of two professionals other than clerical staff. Most branches have only amateur administrative staff.

History. The CPRE was founded at the end of 1926. A preliminary meeting was held on the premises of the Royal Institute of British Architects. It was addressed by Neville Chamberlain, then Minister of Health (and therefore in charge of planning). Those present included

Sir Guy Dawber and Sir Patrick Abercrombie, perhaps the two most respected planners of the day. Indeed, it was Abercrombie's essay, 'The Preservation of Rural England' in the *Journal of the Town Planning Institute* which had provided the intellectual impetus behind the movement. Chamberlain's speech envisaged the CPRE as a 'co-ordinating' body for organisations and individuals interested in educating and rousing the public and actively protecting the landscape. 'Deeply though the English people love their land', the minister argued, 'it was threatened by lack of thought and organisation.'

Until the war the CPRE remained largely as a propaganda group, arguing against tasteless ribbon development and acting as a 'ginger group' for the ideas of preservationist planning in general and National Parks in particular. After the war, the role changed radically. The 1947 Town and Country Planning Act and the 1949 National Parks and Access to the Countryside Act, together with the policies for green belts and Areas of Outstanding Natural Beauty and also the preservationist values incorporated into development planning, were responsible for this change. No longer had the Council any major legislative aims. Furthermore, after 1947, there was far more that they could actually do, at both local and national level. Public bodies now had far more control over the environment; so to influence them was a much more fruitful exercise. The style of disputes and propaganda changed, becoming more sophisticated and less bitter. Before the war there were no rules to the planning game; by 1949 it was becoming a skilled game with known rules and players who understood one another.

In many respects the situation which emerged then remained until the 1970s, but there were signs of change from the late sixties. The pressures for change consisted mainly of the broader scope and conception of contemporary arguments about conservation. There was some change away from concentration on the details of cases and back to aggregative propaganda. In 1969, the name was changed from C. Preservation R.E. to C. Protection R.E. and the constitution revised. In the same year, in November, the Council was involved with the 'Countryside in 1970' Standing Committee (of which it was a constituent body) and the Council for Nature (one of its own constituent bodies) in setting up COENCO (Committee for Environmental Conservation), a broad co-ordinating body without individual membership. It is a body which seeks to act as a forum for information and discussion only, but the subject matter of its sub-committees—on pesticide pollution, water pollution, air pollution and noise—are indications of an increasing concern with aggregative change.

Membership. Because of its structure, no meaningful figure can be given for CPRE membership. There are about 4,000-6,000 direct

H*

subscribers to the Headquarters Group and 15,000-20,000 subscribers to branches. The most realistic picture of the nature of activists can be taken from the list of Chairmen and Secretaries of county branches:

House of Lords	7	19%
Justice of the Peace or civil honour	13	16%
Relevant technical qualifications	13	16%
Other academic qualifications	8	10%
Military rank	25	31%
Males with none of the above	21	26%
Females with none of the above	10	12½%

Note: 'Relevant technical qualifications' also includes membership of associations in the fields of law, architecture, planning and surveying.

Even from this relatively small sample and superficial evidence a picture emerges: activists of the CPRE as such tend to have either a high social status or some expertise in a field related to planning. A number of hypotheses can be suggested to explain the high proportion of military ranks: many non-professional officials are retired and thus belong to a generation with a high proportion of ex-soldiers, the CPRE is associated in many areas with the traditional 'county' establishment, there is some association of aspiration between the army and the land. The twenty-five included twenty-three army officers, no RAF.

A slightly different picture emerges if we consider the thirty-one members of the Executive Committee plus the five full-time administrators:

House of Lords	6	17%
Civil honours	11	30%
Relevant technical qualifications	8	22%
Other academic qualifications	6	17%
Military rank	3	8%
Males who list none of the above	9	25%
Females who list none of the above	1	3%

An examination of the lists of branch subscribers shows a similar picture: a high proportion of JPs, double-barrelled names and members of historically important families. It would be wrong to describe CPRE activists as 'middle-class', they are upper and upper-middle class in a large part. Though one assistant secretary at Head Office assured me that: 'Some of our members are even lower than middle-class.' Certainly, the Council is linked through its constituent bodies with groups which have a relatively high proportion of working-class members: the Ramblers and Youth Hostels Associations as well as Labour-dominated councils.

Ideology. The 1969 Constitution of the CPRE states the aims of the organisation in the context of statistics about environmental change, emphasising figures about the urbanisation of rural land. 'The aim of the CPRE', it says, 'is to ensure that not a single acre is lost through greed or neglect.' They have never argued against economic growth; they have only tried to civilise it. Formally, and informally, at every level, the CPRE operates within the administrative culture.[3] Most CPRE activists, particularly professionals, have no clear criteria for distinguishing an important issue and certainly no theory of man and environment. Moderation and empiricism are general facets of the approach.

Three recent Chairmen of the CPRE have been members of different political parties: Lord Birkett (Liberal), Lord Molson (Conservative), and Lord Kennet (Labour). It would be difficult to generalise about the balance of political views in the organisation, but the two most common types are 'Fabian' Labour and 'paternalistic' Tory. 'Business' Tories and 'trade union' Labour are, not surprisingly, poorly represented.

Finance. Financial assets are very little guide to the resources of the CPRE: it can often do quite expensive things very cheaply. One example at national level: in 1970 from a total expenditure on the M40 inquiry of £2,570, £2,400 was reimbursed by the ministry. The Lancashire Branch persuaded the planning consultancy firm of Colin Beck and Partners to prepare without charge a report on the Cartmel area. This report enabled them to press effectively for the designation of the area as a Conservation Area under the 1968 Civic Amenities Act. Such a report would otherwise have cost in excess of £5,000.

In 1970 investment and other income allowed the Headquarters Group to have an expenditure of £27,330 while the Lancashire Branch had an expenditure of just under £7,000. One important financial advantage is 'Registered Charity' status which means that donations and subscriptions are allowable against tax: individuals can give money to the Council which would not otherwise be theirs, but the Government's.

Activities. Decisions affecting CPRE principles emerge from many institutions: at national level, from Parliament, from ministries (chiefly, but not exclusively, from the Department of the Environment), and in effect from public inquiries. At local level many decisions emerge (particularly since 1968) from the planning departments: others have to be seen in terms of the Planning Committee and its sub-committees. There are also group activities which do not constitute attempts to influence 'decisions' as such, but which are intended to shape the whole context of policy: campaigns to influence public opinion, for instance, or attempts to persuade firms to spontaneously modify their projects.

At national level the CPRE is always preparing information and arguments about policy for informal use in negotiations with the Civil Service and, where politically and administratively appropriate, for more public use in Parliament. Similarly, at Branch level there is a constant process of negotiation and consultation with the local planning authority. This includes informal contact between the Secretary, Stanley Jeeves, and the Chief Planning Officer, Aylmer Coates. Such is the respectability of the CPRE in Lancashire that they are formally represented on the county council's countryside sub-committee of the planning committee, and Aylmer Coates is himself a member of the Branch. Indirect Branch pressures include propaganda and 'education' campaigns such as the film about the Furness District, 'Over the Sands', which was seen by more than 100,000 people.

A combination of both levels may be required for more dramatic activities, such as fighting major cases. The struggle over the Manchester Water Order on Ullswater and Windermere, for instance, lasted from 1961 to 1966, cost the CPRE £11,000, and involved local planning authorities, both Houses of Parliament, a special conference, a public inquiry, two ministries, and (finally) the Cabinet. The CPRE claim a '75 per cent' success in that the two lakes had to be landscaped with the level maintained, the quantity of water was limited, the scheme was subjected to loan sanctions, and the plan for a visible pipeline was prohibited. At the same time, promises were given by the minister that nothing more would be extracted from Ullswater and that there would be no artificial reservoirs in the area.

The Overall importance of the CPRE. The Council has no sanctions, except possibly an appeal to the tasteful horror of educated opinion which might conceivably swing votes. It is well-endowed with other resources including a sympathy in widespread social values (especially those of decision-makers) which make it embarrassing to oppose the CPRE and virtually impossible to condemn it. It is well served in terms of contacts and expertise, giving it an ability to communicate evaluations and ideas through effective channels and have them taken seriously. Furthermore, it has no permanent countervailing pressures; no group exists which is primarily concerned to oppose its principles.

However, if we consider two extreme hypotheses—firstly, that the CPRE has had little impact on environmental planning in England and, secondly, that in any drive through the English countryside, the impact of the CPRE is present—neither can be easily dismissed.

There are both conceptual and practical difficulties of assessment both of particular cases and of overall impact. In the first place, the CPRE as an emphasis group shares so many values and ideals with the public bodies on which it puts 'pressure' that it becomes difficult to detach achievements of the group from achievements of certain planners or planning ideals. This problem is exacerbated by CPRE tactics. Except in extreme cases (in which Manchester Corporation and the Central Electricity Generating Board seem often to figure), the norm is to attempt to negotiate satisfactory solutions with the bodies concerned, especially where they are public bodies. Stanley Jeeves argues that: 'Fighting cases means publicity. Publicity means conflict, and conflict can mean loss of contacts and credibility.' Often neither side in an environmental issue (just as in a wages issue) is prepared to say what they really mean; the CEGB has been accused of putting forward plans which are extremely damaging to the landscape in order to 'soften up' the conservation groups. When this happens, and both sides think they have beaten the other, there are practical difficulties to finding out what has really been achieved. In any case, it is difficult to distinguish between the impact of an organisation, the impact of the social group or groups corresponding to that organisation, the impact of individual activists (not necessarily dependent on the existence of the organisation or group), and the effects of those social values which constitute the basic purposes of the organisation. So we must be careful when we say 'the CPRE' to distinguish the effects of the organisation from other effects. Finally, there is an additional difficulty because in any important matter the CPRE has a plethora of allies; it works in conjunction with other private and public bodies. In the Manchester Water Order case, for instance, it worked in conjunction with the National Trust, the Friends of the Lake District and a dozen other bodies. Crediting 'effective pressure' to one body rather than another simply cannot be done in any precise way.

Despite these difficulties, my own assessment is that the CPRE, even conceived rigidly as an organisation, has had a great impact on planning. This impact can be seen partly in the prevention of development, particularly in the National Parks and Areas of Outstanding Natural Beauty. But mainly it should be seen in the standards of taste which have been imposed on developments as large as the M6 and as small as village bridges. These standards may be second nature to the better planning departments now, but it is doubtful whether they would have prevailed if it were not for the CPRE.

THE CONSERVATION SOCIETY[4]—A DIFFERENT KIND OF PRESSURE

The Conservation Society is a creature of a different age from the CPRE. The environmental fears and preoccupations are different, too. It was founded in 1966 'for public educational purposes'. A statement of aims in the Conservation Society *Newsletter* of November-December

1971 distinguishes between three: 'the conservation of resources, the care of the environment, reduction in pollution and population'. Like the CPRE it can claim supporters affiliated with all three parties; its survey of its own membership claimed 'approximately 51 per cent unaffiliated, 19 per cent Conservative, 15 per cent Labour, 15 per cent Liberal'. It has had, at times, parliamentary supporters in all three parties, including Sir David Renton (Conservative), Dr Edwin Brooks (Labour) and Dr Michael Winstanley (Liberal).

But here the similarity ends, for the commitment to a reduction in population has put the organisation outside of established values. One consequence of this has been the refusal of the Charity Commissioners to allow Registered Charity Status on the grounds that the organisation was 'too political'. The preoccupation with population rather than other aims has increased with the development of the Society; at the 1971 Annual General Meeting, eight of the twelve resolutions were about population policy.

The Society does not have influential contacts like those of the CPRE. Nor does it want to, for it seeks to influence certain aggregate variables (population and economic growth), firstly by direct social action and secondly by changing the context of policy-making through changing public opinion. Direct social action includes attempts to convert individual doctors to a 'liberal' attitude to contraception and abortion.

I suspect the Conservation Society represents something radically different from the CPRE: viz. an academic, non-religious, scientifically aware fear of the kinds of change which may happen in the last quarter of the twentieth century. In their publicity leaflet, they say of themselves: 'As regards religion, we also have a large proportion of uncommitted people, but our membership includes followers of all the main religious faiths.'

A breakdown of officers, including Vice-Presidents, in 1969 (total 32) shows:

Titles	5	15%
Doctors	5	15%
Professors	10	30%
Civil awards	7	22%
None of these	5	15%

In this case, too, there are enormous difficulties in assessing effects, particularly in distinguishing the effects of individuals from those of the group. As an organisation, according to Stephen Lawrence, the Chairman, they aim only to act as a 'catalyst'. They may have done so, even though their part cannot be estimated, in that they have been part of the mysterious process through which population policy and control, 'unthinkable' in the mid-1960s, became respectably 'thinkable' by the mid-1970s.

NOTES

1. W. J. M. Mackenzie, 'Pressure Groups in British Government', in Richard Rose (ed.), *Studies in British Politics* (London, Macmillan, 1967), p. 207.
2. For this account I have used the ephemera, the monthly and bi-monthly, *Bulletin* and the *Annual Reports* of the CPRE national organisation and the *Annual Report*, the magazine *Countrywise*, and ephemera of the Lancashire Branch. I am most grateful to Miss J. C. Revel and Mr Patrick Daly, former officers in Head Office, and to Mr Stanley Jeeves, Secretary of the Lancashire Branch, for the time they have spent talking to me.
3. H. E. Bracey, *Industry and the Countryside* (London, Faber, for the Acton Society Trust, 1963), says: 'In this country it is not a realistic policy to oppose all objectionable developments and the Council appears to be, above all else, a realistic body.'
4. I have used Conservation Society ephemera as well as the *Newsletter* and the magazine *Conservation*. I am most grateful to Mr S. G. Lawrence, Honorary Secretary of the Society, for the time he spent talking to me.

Chapter 11

Visionary Planning

In this book I have been critical of planning in Britain, especially its intellectual coherence and assumptions. However, I hope I have also been properly appreciative of the planning system; it has made life better than it otherwise would have been for many people in many ways. So I stand to be attacked from two opposite sides: by those arguing that my criticisms are ideological or pay insufficient attention to the complexities and difficulties of planning and by those who argue that my favourable appreciation of the system shows a lack of imagination as to what might have been achieved.

An extreme version of the latter criticism might claim that British 'planning' has not been planning at all, but mere negative control. Its achievements fall well below the achievements of (say) Swedish planning and well below the aspirations of its founding fathers (whether Geddes and Howard in the earlier period or Abercrombie and Sharp in the later). The system has never encouraged truly creative planning; it has even lost the aspiration to create new landscapes and new lives. One reason for this failure, it could be argued, has been the inability of the system to surmount the obstacle of property rights; the practical form in which planners face this problem is in the difficulty of purchasing land for development. Indeed, many readers may be surprised that I have paid so little attention to the problem of land ownership in a book on politics and planning.

I do not accept these arguments either as criticisms of my own emphasis or as criticisms of the achievements of planning. In the first place, I am sceptical about the potential for genuinely creative planning. So are many modern planners: determinism, as the belief that fundamental social improvement can be achieved through architectural change, is no longer a credible premise. Even in the purely aesthetic dimension, I would argue that values change too quickly to inspire confidence in the worth of any orthodoxy. William Wordsworth regarded railways as the ultimate destructive force for the rural scene; later the steam train was seen by many as a natural complement and addition to the English countryside.[1] Thomas Sharp regarded Victorian architecture as the ugliest feature of the English landscape; he extolled straight lines and white materials.[2] Now many people react strongly against the architectural tradition which he helped establish and there is a growing cult, in the wake of John Betjeman, of Victorian architecture. In any case, there is a certain amount of comprehensive environmental creation in the system—most clearly in the New Towns—and it has by no means furnished environments undeniably superior to combinations of control and organic growth. Negative, partial planning is on safer ground; it can, at least, rely on the preservation of environments which have stood the tests of time and changing judgements to provide the context for new development. In Britain, by common consent, we are not really in the business of developing brand new environments and life-styles.

I am doubtful, too, about the importance of property in planning. The essential dilemmas remain whatever the system or distribution of land-ownership; conservationist groups in this country expend more energy struggling against Manchester Corporation, the CEGB, the Ministry of Transport Industries, and other *public* enterprises than they do against private enterprise.[3] Their complaints about environmental evaluations are echoed by those of Alexander Solzhenitsyn about development in the Soviet Union. There are the same issues in the Soviet system of public land as in the British system of publicly controlled land which is (mainly) privately owned.

Any interesting conclusions about the planning process must involve value-judgements. It is orthodox in the study of society to insist that value-judgements be kept separate from non-evaluative analysis. I intend to do this by putting my heart on my sleeve and stating certain premises clearly. Firstly, I believe that environmental beauty is very important, at least as important a criterion for planning as economic efficiency or social progress. Secondly, I am a conservative; I believe that rapid change is generally bad in its effects. 'Change' here includes demographic growth, rapid economic growth, rapid inflation, and social or political change involving rapid upheavals of role or status. Many people are conservatives in this sense, but conservatism has found few expressions as an explicit ideology; very broadly, the influential ideological traditions of the developed world are progressive. They emphasise the benefits, rather than the disbenefits, of change; the generalisation extends to explicit capitalist ideology, to Marxism and to social democracy. The articulate and genuinely conservative ideologists include J. S. Mill, Mishan and Solzhenitsyn. I should add that conservatism is by no means the same as emphasis on ecological balance, but it does come to many of the same prescriptive conclusions. Both stress the disadvantages of rapid economic and demographic growth; both warn that choosing change may have consequences which are both unpleasant and unforeseen. The difference is that ecologism (if I can call it that) is about survival whereas conservatism sees itself as one choice among alternatives. To extend an analogy I used earlier, ecologism concerns itself with keeping the car on the road, conservatism with choosing a pretty route.

Extreme environmental conservatism would be a social policy designed to prevent any increase in population or urbanisation, and all economic growth which threatened to reduce the quality of the environment. Such conservatism would, of course, be a radical and unorthodox doctrine. I would propose a more moderate conservatism, arguing that extreme conservatism is almost a self-contradiction. Although change cannot be prevented, some things can and should be preserved. I choose the word 'preserved' deliberately and for two reasons. It is a clearer word than 'conserved', which has a tendency to slide between being equivalent to 'preserved' and having some meaning to do with ecological survival. It is also unfashionable word in our culture and administration; even the CPRE have dropped it from their title. I have argued (in Chapters 7 and 8) that there are no adequately defined totems in our culture, nothing which is regarded as being of absolute value.

The concept of 'totem' derives from the studies of anthropology and psychology. J. G. Frazer defined a totem as:

'. . . a class of material objects which a savage regards with superstitious respect, believing that there exists between him and every member of the class an intimate and altogether special relation. . . . The connection between a man and his totem is mutually beneficient; the totem protects the man, and the man shows his respect for the totem in various ways, by not killing it if it be an animal, and not cutting or gathering it if it be a plant. . . . The clan totem is reverenced by a body of men and women who call themselves by the name of the totem, believe themselves to be of one blood, descendants of a common ancestor, and are bound together by common obligations to each other and by common faith in the totem. Totemism is thus both a religious and a social system. In its religious aspect it consists of the relations of mutual respect and protection between a man and his totem; in its social aspect it consists of the relations of the clansmen to each other and to men of other clans. In the later history of totemism these two sides, the religious and the social, tend to part company. . . .'[4]

I am confident that totemism has something to do with the necessary and proper relationship between a man and his environment: at least a strong analogy, possibly an element of homology. However, the exact nature of the relationship does not matter for my purpose, which is to clarify the principle that environmental planning should involve a large degree of virtually total environmental preservation. As a recommendation this may seem perverse; I have stressed that the planning machinery has had some success in preservation and yet my main prescription is more preservation. My preservation, though, would be on a more clear-cut totemistic basis. It would make plain and public the areas to be preserved and the rigidity (within reason) with which they were to be preserved. I hope that such a policy would go some way to cure what I can only call 'environmental neurosis'; by this, I mean the constant fear that one's environment is about to be destroyed, the worrying belief that nothing is safe from change and decay. I believe that only if environmental neurosis is cured can we begin to enjoy the artefacts of the twentieth century. I like the Rugeley 'B' power station, the steelworks of Margam and Rotherham, 'Spaghetti' Junction in Birmingham, and the northern section of the M6 motorway between Preston and Carlisle. I can find neon lighting, concrete bridges and motor cars very beautiful. But when I express these preferences and judgements they are often received with scorn, derision or disbelief. I am convinced that this is not because of my own aesthetic eccentricity, but because most people cannot see the artefacts of their own time except as a threat to their environment. With effective and properly publicised totemistic planning, the threat would be removed. This would have a constructive effect: people would be able to see the advantages and possibilities of modernity. Not only would public and private enterprises initiate more interesting projects, they would also meet less passionate opposition from 'conservationists' who feel they must protect everything because nothing is sacred. Totemism is thus superior to Benthamism primarily in its psychological effects. Benthamism implies incrementalism: all environmental decisions must be treated on their preference—achieving merits at every stage. Totemism not only allows a far greater sense of security, but also greater creativity.

SUBSTANTIVE ENVIRONMENTAL TOTEMISM

It is the duty of anyone who advocates a new principle for policy to outline how it should be effected. I would divide the application of my principle into three parts:

1. *The National Parks.* There are at present over 5,000 square miles of National Park in England and Wales. The total area should be increased to include more of the Pennines and Wales, but to 8,000 square

miles at the most. They should be administered by independent bodies responsible to central government, though these bodies should be required to consult relevant local authorities and must contain representatives of the authorities. Their policy should be to prohibit all development, including tourist development, which might change the character of the area. The administrative bodies should aim to control and reduce the number of motor vehicles in National Parks and on no account should allow road development. Our National Parks are still large and attractive if one travels on foot or on horseback; they are not large for the motorist and they are not attractive when congested by motor vehicles and caravans. Of the many ways of achieving this I prefer the simple one of charging admission at a toll-gate (with passes for residents and goods access). I regard this as a solution which is administratively cheap and easy, which maximises individuals' freedom of choice, which will, to some extent, limit the number of vehicles and which will provide a revenue for the parks taken from those who use them deleteriously. The money can be used to finance a fuller wardening service for maintaining and improving the parks and for subsidising public transport to and from urban centres and within the parks.

2. *Areas of Outstanding Natural Beauty.* These at present cover something under 4,000 square miles. There could be some increase, but the most important thing is to ensure their strict preservation. They should remain under the immediate jurisdiction of the local authorities who should be equipped with greater control, particularly over agricultural uses. Footpaths should be re-opened and created, but there should be no other positive action.

3. *The Preservation List.* There already are Conservation Areas, 'listed' buildings, National Trust properties, tree preservation order, Country Parks, Nature Reserves, Forest Parks, Crown Lands and many other categories of administrative preservation. My plan is to co-ordinate them all—and add to them—by means of a list in the Department of the Environment. The Preservation List would include every sort of area; indeed, variety would be the clearest principle of selection. It would contain the names of woods, streets, areas of towns, parks and areas of every kind of landscape, all of which were to be strictly preserved by local authorities in accordance with central policies. Country parks and other features (such as lakes and canals) of recreational importance would be listed, but there should be a clear distinction between features preserved for an active recreational pursuit and those which are primarily to be looked at. Further land should be added to both parts of the list, but the most important achievement would be

clarifying and co-ordinating so that, for instance, a Londoner could look at the Home Counties edition of the list and know where he could find woods, water to sail on, nature walks or areas of Georgian housing. Most importantly, the list should include a variety of industrial areas (restored in many cases) because these are scarcely catered for in the present machinery and I believe that future generations will value them.

These measures are not intended to supersede planning as it now exists. The most radical, the Preservation List, would require a great deal of public money to have much effect. All three proposals involve staff being employed in the administration of preservation, particularly if we are to cross a psychological barrier and convince people that their environment is actually improving. However, the sums involved would not be large by the standards of central government expenditure. Nor do my proposals imply that large amounts of productive land will cease to be productive. Even a maximal assumption of land in each category would not add up to the 40 per cent of land in England and Wales estimated as being preserved in 1963. In any case, most preservation involves continuation of the existing use; only future development is prevented.

'GROWTH'

Sustained economic growth must in the long run destroy our environment and be to the detriment of all men. However, the long run may be longer than we need contemplate; I believe that neither demographic growth nor economic growth seriously threaten the environment of Britain at the moment. Provided they are sufficiently constrained by policy we need not feel threatened by either. Economic growth is not necessarily an environmental evil, but neither am I convinced that it is much of a human benefit in developed countries. There is a great deal of evidence that the satisfaction human beings obtain from possession of material objects is largely comparative: the objects themselves mean nothing; it is only as sources and symbols of status and self-esteem that they satisfy. If this is the case, then prosperity has the odd property that it is further away the nearer we approach to it. But if this undermines an argument for economic growth, it is not itself an argument *against* growth, only growth-at-all-costs. I think that, in practice, we need growth for preservation. Only with prosperity can we afford an effective maintenance of National Parks or a rehabilitation of historic urban areas or not to develop all our mineral resources. I hope that the discovery of oil in the North Sea may come to be seen as an important cause of Britain's preservation and not its destruction. In any case, it is still possible to hope that the future will be better than the past.

NOTES

1. William Wordsworth, *Guide to the Lakes* (London, Henry Frowde, 1906), 5th edn, pp. 146-66. Wordsworth asked

> 'And must he too the ruthless change bemoan
> Who scorns a false utilitarian lure
> 'Mid his paternal fields at random thrown?'

I should make clear that 'utilitarian' in its ordinary sense in the early nineteenth century meant 'materially productive' by definition and not by implication as it does now.
2. Thomas Sharp, *Town Planning* (London, Penguin, 1940).
3. Alexander Solzhenitsyn, 'Letter to the Soviet Leaders', in *Sunday Times* (3 March 1974).
4. From J. G. Frazer, *Totemism* (1887). Quoted in Sigmund Freud, *Totem and Taboo* (London, Routledge, 1960), pp. 103-4.

INDEX

For Product Safety Concerns and Information please contact our EU
representative GPSR@taylorandfrancis.com
Taylor & Francis Verlag GmbH, Kaufingerstraße 24, 80331 München, Germany